FIRE+ WINE

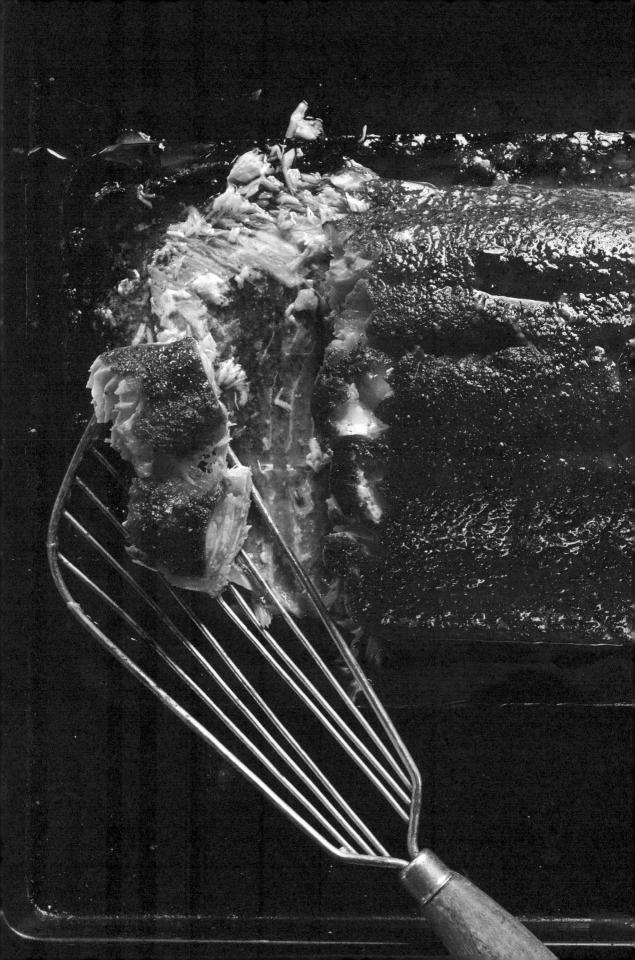

FIRE +
WINE

75 Smoke-Infused Recipes from the Grill with Perfect Wine Pairings

Mary Cressler AND **Sean Martin**

PHOTOGRAPHY BY
Dina Avila

SASQUATCH BOOKS
SEATTLE

CONTENTS

RECIPE LIST

INTRODUCTION

When we first moved to Portland in 2006, Mary unpacked the house while Sean stayed behind in San Francisco for a few weeks finishing up his job. He felt bad that he wasn't able to help unpack much and promised to spend his first few days unpacking the two rooms she had saved for him.

The day he arrived, instead of fulfilling his promise, he spent the entire day researching grills. We couldn't have one in our teeny San Francisco apartment, so he was eager to finally get one now that we had a real backyard. During his second day as an Oregonian, he went shopping, bought a grill, and put it together. The third day we spent grilling.

He didn't get around to unpacking a single box until several days later, despite constant encouragement (read: nagging). Our first grill as first-time homeowners was a standard gas grill. It served its purpose for a short time, but we soon got curious about wood-fired food. Because both of us worked full time (Mary in the wine industry and Sean in insurance), we didn't have much time to dedicate to standing around a smoker, so we opted for a pellet smoker.

We both remember clearly the day we brought it home. The very first things we wanted to cook included strawberries, almonds, salmon, potatoes, zucchini, and chicken. Not quite your typical BBQ fare. But we were curious from day one about how everything would taste cooked on the smoker. We had a lot of mixed results in the beginning and strange reactions from others, such as, "You smoked what?!"

It was a whole new way of thinking about cooking outside, and we were immediately hooked.

It wasn't for several weeks that we even attempted anything that would be considered typical BBQ (pork butt, ribs, brisket, etc.). We were having too much fun seeing how vegetables, fruit, and seafood performed on the smoker. We quickly learned that anything you can cook in your kitchen on your stovetop or in your oven you can cook outside on a smoker or grill, and it's a heck of a lot more fun. Well, most of the time.

The combination of being able to spend time outside, especially in the warm Portland summer months, while cooking together and socializing with our neighbors was such a great bonding experience and a welcome stress relief from our day jobs. Flash forward a few years and we found ourselves living in Connecticut. Our twin boys had just been born, and Mary's wine-industry career transitioned into freelance writing while raising the babies.

As two people who loved going out to eat and exploring new restaurants, we were suddenly forced to cook at home (it's not fun to take two babies out to restaurants, let alone the curious toddlers they quickly grew into).

Instead we spent more and more time determined to make great food at home by homing in on our grilling and smoking skills. Even during several infamous New England blizzards, we used those days off as the perfect opportunity to practice brisket or chicken wings—yes, in the snow.

And while many husbands were watching football and drinking beer on Sundays, Sean spent the afternoon with Mary watching episodes of *BBQ Pitmasters* together while sipping wine.

After three challenging East Coast winters, we were ready to return to Portland but not without adding to the family.

A 16-foot offset commercial smoker, the kind used in competitions and in business settings, is not what most spouses would logically agree to acquire in support of a "hobby," but alas when one of you has a strong dream and vision for the future, the other is (reluctantly) willing to compromise and be supportive (as long as there was wine involved).

And thus "The Beast" was born, aptly named, with the intent to start competing in BBQ competitions (thanks to way too many episodes of *BBQ Pitmasters*). What were we thinking?

That summer we participated in our first BBQ competition. The experience was close to a nightmare. This was mostly because we were rookies and didn't know what the heck we were doing. We also camped out in the Washington desert while others had comfortable trailers. It was hot during the day, cold at night, and during the evening we endured an insufferable windstorm that nearly blew away our tent and kept our fire temperatures inconsistent throughout the night. Oh, yeah, and our then three-year-old boys were with us. Despite our inexperience, our flavors came through and we still placed in the category of Tri Tip. While the experience was less than ideal, we realized then that we were actually homing in on our personal style of BBQ.

That challenge didn't stop us from entering different styles of competitions. One such competition was a national recipe competition, in which we took the grand prize. The recipe? Brisket Nachos, made with a deeply rich chili. What happened next was something we never imagined doing. We started a catering company.

Following that win, Phelps Creek Vineyards in Hood River, Oregon, invited us to serve those award-winning nachos to their guests. We took "The Beast" out to the winery and cooked for a crowd for the first time. It was both terrifying and exhilarating. And apparently, we didn't mess things up, because they asked us to come back again, this time cooking for their wine club. It was at that event that we created our Pinot Noir BBQ Sauce (page 66), using their wine as a base.

Word got out, and we were suddenly doing pop-up and catering events for wineries throughout the Pacific Northwest. In just our second year of catering, we were featured in a cover article in *Oregon Wine Press* about top wine country caterers. Who the heck were we to deserve such honors?!

As we catered more events, we shared many of our recipes on our website, Vindulge, encouraging others to try the recipes themselves. The site gained in popularity, winning awards for photography and nominations from the International Association of Culinary Professionals (IACP) for our recipes and wine pairings. Mary's writing was featured in regional publications as well as prestigious print publications such as *Wine Enthusiast*.

Living and cooking in wine county, we have always made it our goal to create food cooked with wood fire that has wine in mind.

We've been inspired by and have full respect for the classic BBQ regions, such as Texas, Kansas City, Memphis, and the Carolinas. But it's never been our passion. Our passion starts in the Pacific Northwest, where we take what we love about the classic regions and apply them to what we have available here.

Salmon is king here, as are tree fruits and berries of all kinds. Mushroom and truffle country is thriving, and we're surrounded by incredible local ranchers who produce some of the best beef, pork, and lamb we could ask for.

When you start with great ingredients, it's hard not to have great food.

We don't intervene too much when we start with quality ingredients; instead, we let the food speak for itself.

The secret to great salmon starts with good-quality wild-caught fish, seasoned simply with salt and pepper and smoked to the correct temperature. The beurre blanc in the Perfect Smoked Salmon Fillet with Beurre Blanc (page 191) is an added bonus that doesn't take away from the perfectly cooked and incredibly tender fish. It starts with quality fish, and we just don't overcook it. That's it.

There's really no better season than when fresh tomatoes are ripe. We take summer tomatoes and transform them into the most indulgent smoked Bloody Mary mix, smoky marinara sauce, or Smoked Tomato Gazpacho (page 200).

Fresh berries run wild in the Pacific Northwest, and we're constantly using them to add great flavor to sauces, such the topping for the Grilled Cedar Plank Brie and Strawberry Balsamic Glaze (page 72).

Being a caterer in the Portland area also requires adapting to pretty much every dietary need or preference that exists. We've become good at creating vegetarian recipes, for example, that are not only accommodating for those guests who don't eat meat but also taste delicious. The vegetarian Pulled Mushroom Sliders (page 205) are so good you'll forget that there's no meat in them.

Wine writers are given the opportunity to explore wine regions throughout the world, tasting flavors unimagined before. Whenever we return from such a trip, we're inspired to take the best of what we ate and drank from a given trip and adapt the food to wood-fired cooking. The Smoked Pumpkin Risotto (page 221), for example, was inspired by a trip to northeast Italy's Veneto region.

Our hope is that these recipes inspire you to experiment with cooking outside, on your smoker or grill, and try new things, even if it may seem a bit wild (Smoked Honey Butter [page 177] anyone?).

Perhaps you'll be inspired to find something unexpected to throw onto your smoker next time you fire it up.

HOW TO USE THIS BOOK

If there's one thing we recommend, it's to read Fire (page 9) from beginning to end. There you will find the foundations that will give you the tools and confidence to cook the recipes in this book. In that section, we talk about styles of cookers and their benefits, types of fuel and how they work, and how to troubleshoot when things aren't going your way.

Cooking over wood fire is not the same as cooking inside your kitchen. You're competing with several elements and factors that affect cooking time, and you could unknowingly speed up your cooking or slow it down. Understanding how to troubleshoot will create a much more enjoyable experience when cooking outside and give you confidence to take charge.

The biggest and best compliment we receive, over and over, is that our food (whether it's steak, fish, chicken, you name it) is the juiciest and most flavorful that they've ever had. It comes down to two factors: using good-quality meat and cooking it to the perfect temperature. That's it!

When you get comfortable cooking your food to your optimal temperature (and this is going to be different from person to person), the taste of your food will improve immensely.

We also encourage you to start by making a few of the dry rubs to keep on hand as you make your way through the recipes. Homemade dry rubs are easy to make, will last in your pantry for months, and provide great flavor to many of the proteins found in this book.

If you're a wine lover (and we hope you are!), Wine (page 39) will provide a guide to pairing wine with wood-fired food and explain our philosophy for pairing. You think BBQ is just for beer or whiskey? Think again! There's a whole world of delicious wines just waiting for your next wood-fired creations. Pour yourself a glass and get reading.

The food we cook and the wines we drink are not exclusive to the Pacific Northwest. We hope the recipes and wines in this book inspire you to adapt and celebrate the regional cuisines where you live. Above all, we hope you realize that anything you can cook in your kitchen on your stovetop or in your oven you can cook outside on a grill or smoker—and it will be so much more fun to do so!

Cheers, and let's get grilling!

FIRE

Cooking with wood fire is not an exact science. It's more of a craft that you home in on, learning something new each time.

When cooking or baking inside, you are not at the mercy of the elements. When cooking outside, you can't hyperschedule. You do your best to target times, to plan when dinner will hopefully be done. But the reality is that you are cooking with fire, and you are cooking outside. Each time the grill or smoker is used can present different elements, figuratively and literally, that will force you to realize quickly that you have to learn to go with the flow, adjust certain components of your cooking, and modify the day based on what has been presented to you. Our hope is that this section helps guide you through those things, from seasoning to techniques to understanding fire management. As you cook, you will learn how your specific cooker responds to these elements and understand how to modify and adjust to put forth the best results for your family and friends. Your cooker is like a musical instrument; the better you know it, the better you understand its quirks, how to troubleshoot, and how to fine-tune.

If there is one word we would use to describe cooking outside with fire, it is the word *experience*. To be outside with friends and family or to be alone for twelve hours during a brisket cook, everything about cooking outside with fire comes back to the experiences you have and the joy you feel with each and every cook. We hope you can discover not only great food and wine experiences but also the same joy and fun that comes from finishing your first brisket or teaching your child how to manage fire, or creating your own dry rub that wins a competition. Make no mistake; frustration will happen, such as when you feel like you nailed the cook, only to find that the food isn't quite there or is slightly overcooked. That is OK too because you learn from every experience and you use that to improve the next one.

Understanding some basic fundamentals of cooking over wood fire will jump-start your learning curve. So please take the time to read this section and use it as a base of knowledge in your journey.

FIRST THINGS FIRST: GRILLING VERSUS SMOKING

When we say grilling, we are referring to cooking hot and fast, over charcoal or wood. When we say barbecue (or BBQ) or smoking, we are talking about the low heat and slow cooking process that renders meat with amazing flavor due to a combination of heat and wood smoke. We mention this because it matters for technique. You don't BBQ a hot dog; you grill it. You don't grill a large pork shoulder; you BBQ or smoke it.

Your food is done when it is done, not based on an exact measurement of time. In typical recipes, you can generally target a time based upon sauté basics or baking rules. But in BBQ, every cut of meat is going to have slightly different marbling. Your flame may be slightly hotter, or your smoker may be running cooler due to temperatures outside. All these things mean that when grilling and smoking, there are general ranges of time for cooking, but the internal temperature of your meat is the most important indicator of recognizing when your food is done. As you explore low and slow cooking and grilling, your comfort zone will be pushed because you are forced to let go and work with, not against, what nature is throwing at you. That is why you hear the term pitmaster. It's not so much what you are cooking on but instead how you have navigated that day and that cook and put out the best food given the conditions.

SEASONING, INGREDIENTS, AND TOOLS

SEASONING

BRINES: There are two types of brines: a wet brine and a dry brine.

DRY BRINING: This is simply applying salt (or a salty dry rub) directly to the meat, letting it sit overnight, and allowing the process of diffusion to occur. In this process, the salt will be pulled into the meat, moisture pressed out, and then pulled back in, rebalancing that chemical reaction and spreading that flavor and moisture throughout the meat. Brining (dry or wet) is a form of curing.

WET BRINING: A wet brine is a basic mixture of salt and water in which you soak your meat. Through some fun chemistry, the brine is able to add moisture and flavor at the cellular level of the meat. Our base ratio is simply ¼ cup kosher salt to 1 quart water. We then add sugar (¼ cup). When making a brine, you may also add any other flavors you want to include. Taste your brine, as it should taste salty, almost like ocean water.

DRY RUBS: Dry rubs can be as simple as salt and pepper or as complicated as seventeen different ingredients. Dry rubs add a layer of flavor to the exterior of the meat, and if left on long enough and with a salt base, act as a dry brine.

When making a dry rub, we focus on four key elements: sweet, salt, savory, and heat. Each allows you to create a flavor mix that appeals to your palate. You can also use a dry rub as a flavor element in sauces. We will often use it to tie together another element like sauces, mayonnaise, or aioli or mix it into ground meat. Try adding a teaspoon of sweet rub to mayonnaise and see how it transforms the flavor. Throughout this book, you will see our general rubs referenced, but our hope is that you use some of these foundations to experiment and create your own unique combinations.

HEAT: There can be some overlap with savory, but the most common heat elements for our dry rubs will be coarse ground black pepper and cayenne pepper. We buy the coarse ground black pepper in bulk because it is not fun to use a grinder when you need ¼ cup to ½ cup pepper in a rub. Other heat elements can include red chili pepper flakes, although we tend to use those for marinades because they don't dissolve into the meat as finer herb and spice elements do. Other fun heat elements include individual dried chili powders such as ancho and chipotle. We go light on heat to keep the flavors balanced, but if you love that extra kick, experiment with a combination of coarse ground pepper, cayenne, and dried chilis.

SALT: Salt can come in many styles and forms. For dry rubs, the salt we use most is kosher salt (see page 14). Common table salt with iodine is something we just don't use. When using salt, balance the savory and sweet through tasting so you get that salty feel on your tongue but without overpowering your entire mouth. Don't be shy with the use of salt, and be sure to use good-quality kosher salt, such as Diamond Crystal.

SAVORY: This includes dried herbs like sage, thyme, and rosemary, as well as dried spices like paprika, smoked paprika, dried mustard, and chili powder. Granulated garlic, garlic powder, and onion powder are other examples that can overlap and mimic salty flavors. There is a fine line between savory and salt, which is why these savory items and salt complement each other well. If you use chili powder be sure to taste your rub before adding any heat element. Chili powders are a combination of dried chili varietals that can have a heat element as well, and every brand will vary that formula.

SWEET: Sugar is the most common ingredient to add sweetness to a dry rub. Sugar helps to caramelize, especially on long cooks. You can choose from many forms of sugar, from turbinado sugar, which has larger crystals and a light brown sugar component, to dark brown sugar, which has molasses incorporated. When selecting a sugar, we often go to dark brown sugar because it adds more than just sweet; its added molasses deepens the caramelization and is a great offset to heat. When selecting sweet flavor tones, consider whether you plan to grill over high heat. Sugar especially will burn quickly, so for beef or lean cuts that we tend to grill, we avoid or minimize it to prevent flare-ups and a burned flavor.

About Salt

There are many amazing books that go into detail about salt, salt history, and salt techniques. One of our favorites is *Salt: A World History* by Mark Kurlansky, which gives some great insight into salt use around the world. Another is *Salt, Fat, Acid, Heat* by Samin Nosrat, in which she highlights the science and process by which salt interacts with food for flavor elements. Here we want to highlight a few things to consider when reviewing our recipes based on a number of factors, such as: not all salts are created equal.

Kosher salt comes in many shapes and, more importantly, weights. When you see one of our recipes call for 1 tablespoon salt, you have to recognize that the density of that salt will vary from brand to brand. Lay out three brands like Morton's Kosher, Diamond Crystal Kosher, and Jacobsen Kosher, and you will see the crystal sizes are very different. If you weigh them, you will also see that they weigh different amounts by volume. We like Jacobsen Kosher and Diamond Crystal and use them both. We suggest you find a kosher salt you like, stick with it, and feel comfortable in adjusting the salt measurement based on your flavor preference. The recipes in this book were created using Diamond Crystal.

Finishing salts are another great way to add a touch of salinity as we serve our food. Finishing salts tend to be sea salts that can vary in texture but most commonly have a grainy or squared crystal component. They are delicate and very light. Using a finishing salt allows us to go light on salt in the early seasoning when cooking for a crowd, so that those with more salt sensitivity can season to their taste. They are also great for topping appetizers or a simple slice of bread with butter.

We don't use iodized or table salt. The flavor from kosher and finishing salts gives us everything we need with—what we feel—is a purer salt flavor.

MARINADES: Marinades are a way to introduce flavor to any cut of meat or protein. They are best as a combination of liquids with added flavor elements like herbs, vegetables, or dry rubs. The marinating process is important to balance the liquids so your marinade doesn't come across as overly oily or overly acidic. Marinating tenderizes meats that may be tough and have a lot of muscle fiber. It also incorporates flavor into the protein versus a rub, which tends to simply flavor the outside of the meat. You want to be careful not to overmarinate because then you start to lose the flavor of the meat. This timing will vary from cut to cut. Fish, for example, barely needs an hour to marinate, while beef can handle a few hours and poultry can handle overnight.

SAUCES AND GLAZES: Sauce is often synonymous with BBQ, but the words *sauce* and *glaze* are interchangeable. It's more about the application, so don't get too caught up in one versus the other. We use a glaze to brush onto meat while it is still cooking, with the intent that it will caramelize as the meat continues to cook.

The BBQ sauce most people think of is a tomato and molasses style associated with Kansas City. But we think there are lots of ways to create sauce. It can have a berry or vinegar base, and it can contain mayo, or even relish. Living in the Pacific Northwest, we are surrounded by fresh fruit, berries, and wine, so our sauces are going to reflect the bounty around us. The key is that the sauce isn't the main star; the protein is. Your sauce is simply that condiment you use on the finished product.

INGREDIENTS

Technique and seasoning are key ways to achieve great-tasting food. But we firmly believe where everything really starts is in the quality of meat you select. The United States Department of Agriculture (USDA) inspects meat. The decision whether to rate meat is made by the rancher. That is important to know as you select your meat because you can have incredible cuts of meat from farmers that aren't officially rated by the USDA.

BEEF: Marbling is key with beef. Yes, the breeds of cattle can help, but no matter the breed, what you want to see in beef are the fine white striations of fat that interweave with the muscle otherwise referred to as intramuscular fat.

FREE-RANGE GRASS-FED: This is not a rating, but be aware that the lack of a grain feed and having been pasture raised only mean that the marbling and flavor will be slightly different. We tend not to use 100 percent grass-fed cattle for brisket, for example, because we want a lot of marbling. But for a grilled steak, it can be a nice option. Grass-fed cows tend to have a different flavor profile than feed-based cows. Some ranchers will raise on pasture and then finish with a grain feed as well to balance the two.

LOCAL: It is important to know that your local ranchers may elect not to pay for a rating, although they will have been inspected. As you look at hyperlocal ranchers, look for that intramuscular fat, which may be

Prime-worthy but just not rated as such. We have some great local ranchers in our area that we source meat from. Not all of them have meat that is rated, though the quality is easily on par with top-third Choice or Prime.

USDA RATING: You will see USDA quality gradings of Select, Choice, and Prime. These ratings identify levels of marbling, with Select having the least amount and Prime having the most marbling. Within the three ratings, there are top, middle, and bottom ratings as well. So, you can get a top-third Choice steak that borders on Prime. There is a big price difference in those gradients.

WAGYU: Wagyu beef represents specific breeds of cattle from Japan. When you see Wagyu in the United States, it is most likely American Wagyu or American Kobe beef, in which the Wagyu cattle were brought to the United States and bred with angus breeds. These cuts, while expensive, will represent some of the most marbled. Wagyu has its own rating system of three to twelve, with three representing little to no intramuscular fat and twelve representing the highest level of intramuscular fat. This rating system is separate from the USDA system. With various brands, the producers may market their Wagyu-style beef with their own system like five-star, gold, or reserve. But the marbling is key, and often those will reference back to the three to twelve rating.

LAMB: Lamb is juvenile sheep or sheep up to a year old. Lamb can be rated Prime and Choice. Marbling is again the key differentiator. When you hear spring lamb, that indicates the timing of when the lamb comes to market since all lamb would be less than a year. As lamb ages, it is referred to as mutton.

PORK: Pork is not rated in a USDA system. As with beef, the intramuscular fat in pork is important for flavor. Regardless of the breed, an eye on marbling is important. A Berkshire or Korubota pork tends to have higher marbling versus lesser-known pork breeds. You can see the theme: it's all about the marbling and that you can see right away.

POULTRY: Poultry has a grading level, but it is uncommon to see anything other than A-level poultry in a store. Instead of a USDA rating, we tend to look for free-range organic poultry, in which the birds are allowed to forage as naturally as possible, are fed organic feed (with no pesticides), and are free of antibiotics or hormones.

Pantry Essentials

BREAD CRUMB: Panko is our preferred bread crumb.

BUTTER: We use unsalted butter to control how much salt goes into a dish.

FLOUR: If using flour, we use all-purpose.

MAYONNAISE: Mayo with few ingredients is our preferred option. When making from scratch, it's oil, lemon juice (or vinegar), and egg yolks. We try to make homemade whenever we can.

MOLASSES: We use blackstrap, given the flavor intensity.

MUSTARD: Dijon mustard originates from Dijon, France. We use Dijon-style mustard as it has good-quality white wine in it and great acidity. Grey Poupon is our preferred Dijon mustard.

OLIVE OIL: The flavor of olive oil can change with the variety of olive and the freshness of the oil. We use extra-virgin, cold-pressed olive oil as a starting place for flavor and better quality. We try to find the freshest oil we can, and use it within one year of pressing.

TOOLS

BLUETOOTH THERMOMETER: It is worth getting a two- or four-zone Bluetooth thermometer. By zone, we mean that you have two or four probes you can connect to one monitor. For example, on a brisket cook, you can measure the temperature of the grill and the brisket for two-zone measurements. For a big cookout, you can measure the smoker and monitor your chicken, brisket, and pork shoulder for four zones. This allows you to transmit to your mobile device the temperature of the meat as well as the ambient temperature of the smoker so you won't have to open the smoker or grill and lose precious heat.

CEDAR PLANK: Planks of wood are a great way to add smoke to high-heat grilled meats. They're great used on gas grills for almost any meat cooked, and add an incredible flavor to any fish.

CHIMNEY STARTER: Using a chimney starter is a fast way to concentrate heat and light charcoal without the use of lighter fluid. Simply add paper to the chimney starter under the charcoal and light it. Charcoal will be hot and ready for grilling in as little as twenty minutes.

Food Temperature

Unlike the recipes in traditional cookbooks with clear timelines, in this book every cut of meat is going to cook a little differently. Even the smallest variation in the size or marbling of two rib-eye steaks (well-marbled versus lean) will make a difference in the exact time it will take for them to cook and come to perfect temperature. You have to let go of the traditional idea of how things cook in the oven (45 minutes in the oven at 375 degrees F and it's done) and instead recognize that temperature is the truth for determining when meat is done. There will be some consistency in time; for example, we know a tri tip or salmon fillet will be done in about an hour. But the precision within that hour requires checking at 40 minutes and then monitoring the temperature until it's done to personal preference and safe to eat.

The USDA publishes a target for the minimum cooking temperature for a variety of cuts. What is important to know is that the USDA has adjusted its targets over the years (pork is a great example), and it is generalizing the safe-zone temperature with little consideration of where the meat comes from. Over the years, we have realized that as we have built relationships with our meat butchers and suppliers, we have adjusted our own target temperature ranges because we know how the meat was raised and processed. If you want to be sure you are cooking to the minimum temperature per USDA or consider yourself at risk for potential foodborne illnesses, be sure to cook the meat to the USDA minimum.

Carryover cooking refers to when the meat is removed from the heat source and the meat continues to cook. For smaller cuts, this can be 3 to 5 degrees F, for larger cuts, 5 to 8 degrees F. We remove the meat at the lower temperature so it can come up in temperature while resting.

MEAT	USDA SAFE ZONE (IN DEGREES F)	OUR TARGET (IN DEGREES F)
Beef (ground)	160	160
Beef (steaks)	145	125
Fish	145	130
Lamb	145	130
Pork (whole)	145	135
Pork (ground)	160	160
Poultry (chicken, turkey, game hens)	165	160
Poultry (duck)	165	135
Shellfish	145	135

How you take the temperature of the meat is also important. When using a thermometer, you need to take the temperature in multiple parts of your meat, recognizing the exterior will cook the fastest, while the center and general interior will take the longest. In chicken, insert the probe into the center of both breasts and the thigh. For prime rib, measure the temperature in the center and from the side. For a small steak, bring the probe in from the side, watching the temperature from the entry point and then seeing how it changes as the probe gets closer to the center of the cut. Just coming in from the top in one place won't give you the whole story. You have to insert the probe in multiple locations.

Many, if not all, grills come with their own fixed thermometer to measure ambient cooking temperature. That is helpful as a guide, but that thermometer is measuring only one point in the cooker, which is typically farther away from the heat source. Supplementing that with a probe you can attach to the grill grates is a great way to get the most precise temperature you want for that cook.

IMMERSION BLENDER: Using a blender is a great way to get smooth texture to a homemade sauce or glaze. An immersion blender is a small handheld unit that can be used directly in the sauce pan.

INSTANT-READ THERMOMETER: If there is one single most important tool you should invest in when it comes to cooking over a wood fire, besides your grill or smoker, it is a quality instant-read digital thermometer. A good thermometer takes the guesswork out of it. We use the ThermoWorks's Thermapen Mk4 for general use. It measures the temperature almost instantly (in less than a second), which means you get a precise temperature and can use it to find the coolest part of the meat. Avoid dial thermometers, as they are not as precise.

LARGE SPATULA: We use the Weber Original Wide Spatula. It's great for fish or even large cuts of meat.

LONG TONGS: We use the Weber 6610 Original Tongs, a 20-inch workhorse that allows you to avoid burning yourself over high heat.

MEAT INJECTOR: We use a stainless steel–style meat injector. When looking at options, be sure it comes with replacement O-rings (to keep a strong seal) and is all steel for cleaning easily. There are different head attachments that allow for injecting various marinades or liquids.

NEOPRENE OR NITRILE FOOD-SAFETY GLOVES: When preparing raw meat, be sure to sanitize your prep area after you are done and before moving on to other items to cook. Wearing neoprene food-safety gloves will help avoid cross contamination when handling raw meat.

WATER PAN: We use a metal pan in some of our smokers, which helps keep moisture in the cooker. Not all grills need a water pan, and this is based on personal preference.

TECHNIQUES AND METHODS

TECHNIQUES

SEARING or **MAILLARD REACTION:** The term Maillard (*may-ard*) reaction refers to the chemistry of browning. This is important in grilling because when we use the word *sear*, we are referring to that reaction not just for color but also for texture and flavor. The key to getting that Maillard reaction when grilling is to be sure that water or excess moisture is eliminated. You will see in the recipes that we will add oil to steaks to grill, but it should be a very light coating for allowing the rub to stick to the meat.

REVERSE SEAR: We consider this to be one of the greatest methods to enhance the flavor of any protein. Our reverse sear is modeled after a technique by restaurant chefs who blast a high-heat sear in a pan or flame and then finish the steak in an oven. This prevents burning the meat but still allows it to cook to the perfect final temperature while maintaining a great sear on the outside.

For the reverse sear, we are doing the opposite. We start by smoking the protein at a low heat, allowing the meat to infuse with that sweet smoke, then slowly bring up the temperature in the meat until we get close to the finished temperature. At that point, we remove the protein from the lower heat and finish over a high heat, getting that sear at the end.

RESTING: When you have achieved your desired temperature for a finished meat and removed it from the heat, a couple of things occur. The meat will keep cooking (carryover cooking) and continue to rise in temperature. In addition, the resting period gives the meat (and more specifically the cells in the meat) a chance to cool down. When applying heat, cells expand and push out moisture. If you cut into unrested meat, it will appear moist, but it is like popping a bubble in which the meat will dry out as the moisture is lost on the cutting board. Resting times are a common and important instruction in our BBQ recipes.

Letting a steak rest for ten minutes before cutting into it allows these two things to occur: to finish cooking, usually rising in temperature an extra 5 degrees F, and to start cooling. After the meat finishes cooking off the heat source, the moisture is pulled back into the cells, producing the perfect texture and juicy flavor. This is especially important for long cooks like brisket and pork shoulder, where the resting period is ideally an hour to slowly bring that meat to a good resting temperature. We generally apply a rule of the longer the cook, the longer the resting period.

COOKING METHODS

When using a grill or a smoker, you have to get used to your cooker and develop an understanding of how to set up and maintain your fire. If you have a gas range in your kitchen, you probably have a simmer burner and a boil burner. In the oven, you have the broil and bake functions. On a grill, you have to think of your cooking zones in the same way. Throughout this book, you will see references to these methods.

ONE ZONE OR DIRECT: As the name suggests, this is one cooking zone. Imagine charcoal scattered in one even layer across your grill. This method is great for searing or for fish, vegetables, or anything that cooks hot and fast. But for precision and anything that requires time, the one-zone or direct method can char or burn your protein, especially if there is sugar or high-fat content that can cause flare-ups.

TWO ZONE OR DIRECT/INDIRECT: This is our most common style of setup and you will see it referenced throughout the book. You deliberately have half of your cooking chamber set up with charcoal in an even layer and the other half has nothing. This is important so you can regulate that sear over the hot coal, just like a broiler in the oven, and then quickly move that same piece of meat to the indirect side, which will not flare up or create the potential for the heat to burn your protein. When using a gas grill, the direct or direct/indirect method can be replicated using the burners. If you turn them all on, you have direct. If you turn one or two on and leave a burner off, you replicate the direct/indirect method.

INDIRECT OR OFFSET: This is specific to smoking in which you have a separate chamber, or plate, that will keep the direct heat from searing. It allows you to control lower temperatures so you can focus on smoking, versus grilling, the meat.

GRADIENT: A variation of the direct/indirect method, this is where you have a gradual leveling of your charcoal with one side almost to the grill grates, the center closer to the grill floor, and the far side indirect with no charcoal. This is a great way to maximize space when cooking multiple styles of meat like chicken and beef.

SNAKE: This is a form of indirect cooking that is most commonly used in a kettle grill. Charcoal is the primary heat source, and wood is the flavor. In this case, you line up your charcoal along the outer wall opposite of where the meat is cooking, two or three charcoal lumps stacked. You light one end of the snake with a small number of prelit embers. On top of that charcoal are wood chunks or chips that will combust as the charcoal embers ignite and move down the snake. This allows you to smoke at a low temperature on a kettle grill and is more precise for 200 to 275 degrees F than the standard two-zone or direct/indirect method.

EQUIPMENT

HEAT AND SMOKE

Heat source can be a number of things. The gas grill is one, in which the heat source is the combustion of propane into flame. What we use most often is charcoal, which burns hot and provides a consistent source of high levels of heat.

Another is wood. Think about the campfire that is lit on a cold night as everyone stands around it. Smoke is a by-product of burning the wood. When smoking a brisket, for example, you are making sure to burn wood in such a way so as to release enough smoke to cause the reaction of smoke binding with the cells of the food for imparting flavor. This can be done by combining charcoal with wood, burning wood logs, or feeding wood pellets into an auger with a flame.

CHARCOAL

Charcoal is the most common heat source we use for grilling and smoking. Charcoal comes in a few styles, the most common being lump charcoal and briquettes. Lump charcoal is the most natural form of charcoal and our preferred style, so every recipe you see in this book will assume lump charcoal. It's rough, uneven, and comes in all shapes and sizes. But it burns clean and has a distinct and subtle flavor that you can smell.

Lump charcoal

Briquettes are a form of charcoal that commonly are machined with the use of tools and binding compounds to keep a uniform look and size. Briquettes tend to burn longer than lump charcoal due to their uniform size, but they can transmit unwanted flavors that come from binding and igniting agents.

Whatever you smell coming from the grill or smoker will be imparted into your food. We encourage you to sample and find the charcoal brand that you like best and that is composed of natural ingredients. Avoid chemical additions because you'll likely taste them in your food.

Briquettes

LIGHTER FLUID: Simply put, we don't use it. To us, it is like pouring gasoline on food and lighting it on fire. There are a lot of ways to ignite your charcoal without it. Small starter bricks (not the kind you put into your fireplace), which are often compressed sawdust and wax, are the most common helper we use. The other is a charcoal chimney, in which a cylinder about 12 inches tall is used to focus burning paper or a starter brick under the charcoal and light the charcoal quickly, usually in less than twenty minutes.

WOOD

Because smoke is the key flavor element in BBQ, the choice of wood is important. But where to start? Try the woods that are local to where you live. In Texas, there's post oak and mesquite (among others). In Kansas City, it may be oak and hickory. In the Pacific Northwest where we live, fruitwoods (hardwood) like cherry, pear, and apple are abundant. There are a variety of wood options with specific flavor elements to consider.

> **FRUITWOODS:** Apple, cherry, orange, and pear are examples of fruitwoods that are great for smoking. We love how they pair with fish, pork, and poultry because of the sweet character they offer.

> **NUTWOODS:** Pecan, hazelnut, and almond impart a distinct savory nose that complements fish and wild game like duck.

> **GENERAL HARDWOODS:** Alder, oak, hickory, and mesquite are examples of hardwoods. Use these for beef. The bigger flavor profile lends itself to more campfire characteristics. These we typically use for shorter cooks like tri tip. Some regions love mesquite for long cooks (more than six hours), but we find it adds too much campfire characteristic for our palate and we tend to avoid it.

> **SOFTWOODS:** Cedar is the most common, typically used as grilling planks. But often softwoods do not burn well and when burned have an unpleasant resin flavor that does not lend itself to food. Cedar planks are great for cooking fish, crustaceans, vegetables, and chicken.

Wood is available as chips (small bits of wood, which are best for gas grills), chunks (fist-sized wood chunks you place on top of charcoal to burn), or logs or sticks (split logs often similar in size to what you may put into your fireplace).

GRILLS AND SMOKERS

There are so many variations of grills and smokers on the market. Understanding the pros and cons of each style of grill or smoker will help identify the one that's right for you.

KETTLE GRILL: Let's start with the multitool of grills. The kettle grill is one of the most versatile grills on the market and incredibly affordable. Most don't really think of it as anything other than a grill, but the reality is that it can smoke, grill, and do something in between. We started this journey many years ago on a kettle grill. We mention this because that is truly all you need to get started. Expensive grills and smokers may offer a lot of upgrades to the cooking experience, but fire and heat control, once you've mastered the technique, can be done at an affordable price with a 22-inch kettle grill.

- **PROS**: Affordable; versatile; comes in multiple sizes.
- **CONS**: Heat control not as precise for smoking; may not offer enough room if smoking a large piece of meat.

PELLET GRILL: The pellet grill has evolved over the years. Some don't consider it a "real smoker," but don't let that frighten you. A pellet grill requires the same cooking techniques as any other grill or smoker. It uses food-quality wood pellets as the fuel source, which are stored in a pellet hopper. A motorized auger then pulls the pellets into a firebox, where a hot rod ignites the pellets. Those pellets continue to burn to create smoke and heat. No charcoal and no other wood are needed. Some better manufacturers have setups to do high-heat grilling, although a majority are best for smoking.

- **PROS**: Versatile option for grilling or smoking; no need to manage the fire as you set the temperature on an electric pellet display.
- **CONS**: Wood flavor not as pronounced; difficult to get high-heat searing; cannot use without a power source.

GAS GRILL: Our recipes can be replicated on a gas grill. The direct/indirect method still applies, and you have more control over the burner size for direct grilling.

A gas grill can also smoke. Look for one that has a smoker box built into the unit. Otherwise you will have to use an aluminum foil pouch or an aftermarket cast-iron smoker box to burn wood chips. As a fuel source, use wood chips only, not chunks. If you have a smoker box, put the wood chips into the box, then place the box on the grate directly over the burner. If using an aluminum foil pouch, place the wood chips on the foil and fold to enclose

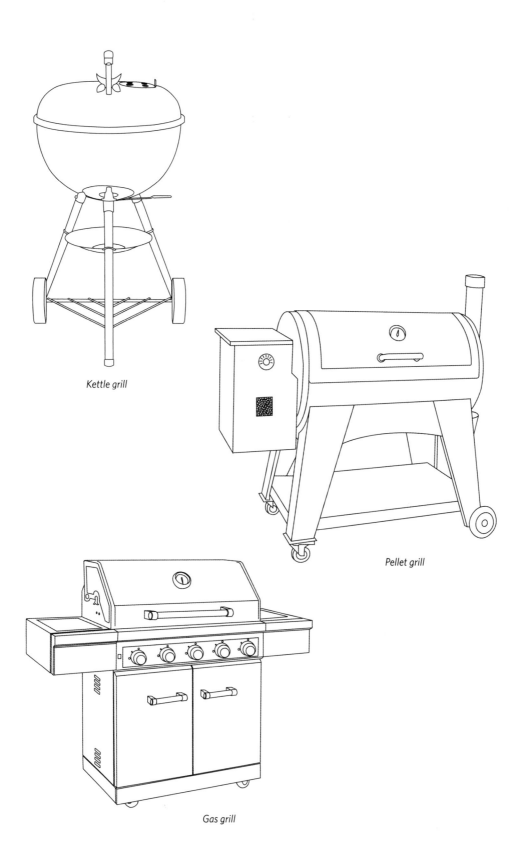

Kettle grill

Pellet grill

Gas grill

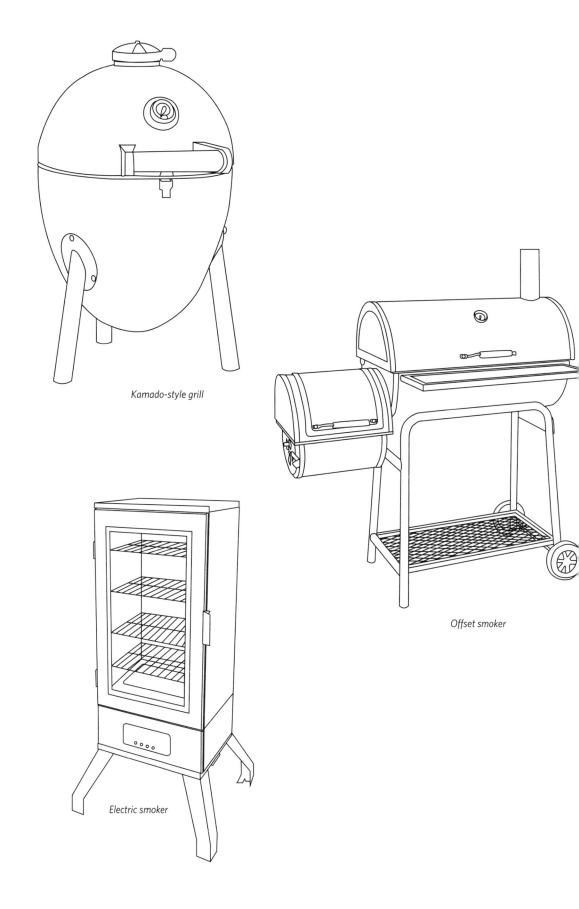

Kamado-style grill

Offset smoker

Electric smoker

the wood chips. With a fork, poke holes in the pouch to release smoke. The burner will heat up the foil pouch or box, burn the chips, and produce smoke. It won't be as easy as using a smoker or grill, but it will add some smoke element. Wood chips can be soaked in water, but that is not necessary.

The other challenge with a gas grill is it isn't built for smoking. A gas grill has a lot of vents, so it is not efficient at holding smoke. This is why it is better to use a cedar plank or consider shorter cooks when smoking.

- **PROS:** Easy to use for high-heat searing; warms up quickly.
- **CONS:** Difficult to use for low and slow grilling and BBQ; not suited for wood burning.

KAMADO-STYLE GRILL AND SMOKER: These are based upon a Japanese style of grill. Typically made of ceramic but also made of steel, these smokers are the most efficient in terms of fuel and wood consumption. The kamado has the balance and ease of a pellet smoker, once you feel comfortable with how to control temperature, as well as provides the natural wood smoke flavor of other more traditional wood cookers. These are so efficient that when you shut down the smoker, the fire is smothered and you can actually reuse the charcoal and wood that has not burned.

- **PROS:** Efficient use of fuel; consistent; can be a smoker or a grill depending on accessories.
- **CONS:** Expensive; very heavy; grilling space can be limited.

OFFSET SMOKER: Offset smokers are just as the name implies. The heat source where charcoal and wood are placed is set off of the main cooking chamber. So it really is built for smoking low and slow, or at temperatures less than 400 degrees F.

- **PROS:** Great flavor profile; a lot of cooking space; great convection.
- **CONS:** Inability to grill at high heat; affordability; the cheaper versions can rust quickly; least efficient in use of fuel source.

ELECTRIC SMOKER: Not be confused with pellet smokers, electric smokers use a heating element to burn wood chips or chunks or sometimes use a gravity-fed fuel system with a heating element. These are affordable and often come in a setup almost resembling a refrigerator.

- **PROS:** Affordable; easy to use for many apartments or smaller spaces.
- **CONS:** Not as much cooking-surface area; does not tend to get hot enough for grilling.

BULLET SMOKER: Bullet smokers offer a little more surface area than kettle grills and often have multiple racks to stack levels of cooking surface. What is nice about a bullet smoker is the ease of access to the fuel source. On a kettle grill, you have to remove the grate. With a bullet grill, you simply open a door and add wood or charcoal without disturbing the meat.

- **PROS:** Easy access to charcoal or wood basin; can stack multiple shelves in larger units; affordable.
- **CON:** Multiple shelves not as easy to access versus other styles.

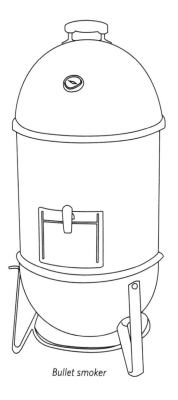

Bullet smoker

FIRE MANAGEMENT

GRILL TEMPERATURE

As a general rule, think of the charcoal as the heat source and the wood element as the flavor source. The more charcoal you have lit and turning to ember, the hotter the fire will be. A large pile of charcoal lit very quickly will generate 400 degrees F or higher of heat; a handful of lit charcoal may only

---

Grill Safety

Too often we see people with grills right along the side of their house. Be sure to consider the worst-case scenario and potential for a grease fire. You want to be sure that the grill is at least 12 inches from the house or, better yet, sitting on the patio or porch away from the home.

Clean your smoker regularly. Pay special attention to grease trap buildup, as that can back up and catch fire. Keep ash out of the firebox—or auger, in the case of pellet smokers—by cleaning after every cook. The best time to clean your grates is after the food is done and the grates are still warm. We clean with a wad of aluminum foil and tongs versus a wire brush, which could lose its bristles in the grill and end up in the food. Simply run the foil along the grill grates to knock off any food residue. Then for the next cook, it is clean and ready to go.

Consider having a fire extinguisher handy, and have it serviced regularly so it's charged.

In the case of a grease fire, the best approach is to smother the oxygen flow to the fire by closing all vents and closing the cover on top of the grill. And of course, call the authorities as needed.

There is a danger zone to be aware of. When smoking, be sure the temperature of your grill is above 140 degrees F (with the exception of cold smoking, which is under 80 degrees F). Per the USDA and most health departments, 140 degrees F is the minimum temperature to avoid the growth of bacteria. This is also important when you are holding cooked food for a long time, waiting to serve. You want to keep that meat in an oven (or in a cooler with no ice) that will maintain the temperature at or above 140 degrees F.

rise to 200 degrees F. Controlling the temperature is important for successful smoking and grilling.

When determining your target cooking temperature, it is difficult to remove heat, so start off with smaller amounts of charcoal. You can always add more to fine-tune or you can adjust the airflow.

Most smokers have dampeners or vents that allow you to control how much air gets into the cooking chamber or firebox. The more air available, the hotter the combustion will be; the less air, the slower and lower the fire will burn. If there is no air, the fire will smother out. Understanding your dampeners and vents is important so you know where to set them for various temperature ranges, especially when smoking at lower temperature. The ideal way to manage dampeners is to allow just enough airflow to create a convection current of air so it circulates in the cooking chamber and draws that smoke around what you are cooking. One general rule is to start your grill with all vents wide open. Then as you see the embers develop and if you add a wood component, you can dial in the vents and close them until you find the right temperature. Be sure to prevent the temperature from going over the desired range; it is much harder and takes longer to pull the temperature down. Instead, look at the temperature gauge; if the desired goal is 225 degrees F, dial those vents almost fully closed as the temperature approaches 180 to 200 degrees F so it slowly comes up to the desired temperature and stays there.

The fire is seeking oxygen to fuel itself, pulling air in and then venting out the smoke, the by-product of the combustion. So, you want to make sure step one is controlling the vents that allow air in. For a kettle grill, these are the vents on the bottom. Then the smoke and heat need to go somewhere to get out. Following this path means there is likely a second stack or vent that pulls or draws the air out. As you control these openings, the air always travels one way or the other. Your goal is to make sure the right amount of air gets to the fire and then out. That's it. As you dial in on your cooker, you will know those ideal settings as you will see the smoke come out. If you see the smoke coming out the wrong end, you aren't opening enough of the exit dampener to pull that air through; it is getting stuck and you get a back-draft. As a general rule, we like our exit dampeners to be open wider than our intake dampeners and then we can dial back from there.

Our recipes always state a target temperature at which to set your grill, even if direct grilling. Let's talk the reality of a grill. You are at the mercy of a lot of factors when maintaining heat and a desired cooking temperature. There will be temperature swings up and down for a host of reasons, such as how hot or cold it is outside, whether it is raining or a sunny, 80-degree day, and what type of fuel is used. All are examples of the complexity of maintaining a desired temperature of the grill. A grill that suddenly spikes from 225 to 250 degrees F is not going to ruin your meat. It just means it will cook a bit more quickly.

Conversely, if you planned for something to be done in two hours at 225 degrees F and it isn't close, do you increase the temperature? Does that influence the meat and flavor? When do you panic? As you get to know your cooker, you will know the best way to dial in temperature. But let's be clear that if you are an hour away from your dinner party with your boss and the meat just isn't close to being done, you can increase the temperature at any magnitude. Want to smoke at 250 degrees F instead of 225 degrees F? That is OK too. It just means the meat will cook faster (most of the time). The key is knowing that once you cross 300 degrees F, you move away from low and slow and enter into grilling territory, losing some of that added smoke flavor.

Temperature Ranges

When considering ranges for smoking versus grilling, we use the following guide. Fahrenheit is also our preferred standard of measurement. Yes, we are based in the United States, but the Fahrenheit scale also provides a little more precision for when to pull your food versus the range in Celsius.

TYPE	COOKING CHAMBER TEMPERATURE (IN DEGREES F)	GREAT FOR
Cold smoking	< 80	Fish, nuts, and cheeses
Smoking	160 to 300	Ribs, pork shoulder, and brisket
Grilling	300 to 500	Burgers, fatty fish, chicken, pork chops, and lamb
Pizza and sear	> 500	Pizza, high-sear lean fish, and most steak cuts

BUILDING AND MAINTAINING A FIRE

For the Kettle Grill

Maintaining a low and slow temperature for multiple hours can seem intimidating. But a few techniques are important to know. Let's focus on a kettle grill as the perfect example. To keep the temperature under 250 degrees F and to get smoke flavor, a steady but small stream of lump charcoal (heat) and wood chunks (smoke flavor) are needed. Adding a small handful of charcoal at a time is inefficient. So the best way is to use the snake method and a charcoal chimney starter.

To do this, create a line of charcoal along the edge of the grill on the opposite side of where the meat will go. Line it right along the metal, and pile three pieces next to each other. Since lump charcoal is not uniform in size, pick pieces that are large and small so they fit together. Continue laying out the charcoal with roughly three next to each other until you have a line of charcoal all along the side of the grill. On top of the charcoal, add the wood chunks every inch.

Adding a small water pan is another opportunity for a kettle grill or offset smoker. Using an aluminum pan or a hotel pan purchased at any restaurant supply store, fill it with water and place it under the meat being cooked. This will add humidity and moisture to the smoker but not take up precious grill space. Moisture is good as it encourages the smoke molecules to bind to the moisture on the meat.

In a charcoal chimney starter, add six to eight coals and light them. Once the coals are all lit or white, dump them in front of the line of charcoal so the lit charcoal is resting on the first set of unlit charcoal. This will light up the snake and be the initial heat element. Place two pieces of wood chunk on the lit charcoal. Add the grill grate and place the lid on the grill.

Now is the time to dial the vents, which are on the top and bottom of the grill. If they are all fully open, it will create the most airflow, making the flame hot and burning the coals faster. If the vents are closed halfway on both the top and the bottom, the airflow is more constricted and the temperature is lower and burning is slower. Get to know the grill and play with the vents. It is always easier to start with the vents nearly closed and then slowly open them to heat up the grill. You can then adjust based on preference. Airflow is still needed to keep the flame going. Is it windy? Then less opening is needed on the grill, or the bottom vent may need to be open more and the top vent almost closed. This is why every cook will be slightly different and it takes practice.

The grill likely has a thermometer built in, but note where it is positioned: at the top of the grill. It is important to have a wireless thermometer that sits on the grate on the indirect side of the smoker. This will give a more accurate reading of the cooking temperature for the meat and can be monitored without removing the top of the grill.

It will take twenty to twenty-five minutes to dial the temperature in the beginning, but as you build comfort with the grill, it will take less time. Mark off the top and bottom vents so there is a reference to the temperature. With the snake method, the grill will last two to three hours with the charcoal and wood chunks. As the charcoal combusts, it slowly reaches the wood chunks, which in turn will combust. This is evident when the smoke comes out of the vent. If cooking longer, simply remove the grill cover, rotate the grill grate, and continue adding charcoal and wood to the unlit side of the snake. For ease, consider grill grates that open along one side to get access to the charcoal.

If high heat is desired later in the cooking process, simply fire up another full charcoal chimney and place the coals into the smoker for grilling. This is great when smoking and then searing at the end.

Line up charcoal and wood in preparation for snake method

For the Pellet or Electric Grill

Pellet grills are controlled by the electronic unit. The colder it is outside, the more pellets are needed to maintain the same temperature. Consider using an insulating blanket when the outside temperature is below freezing, it is made for smokers to increase the grill's efficiency during subfreezing temperatures. Keep the thermometer probe clean. For grilling, it is best to set the pellet grill temperature to high and add grill grates designed for heat distribution, or use cast-iron pans to sear. Water pans are still a good idea.

For the Kamado or Bullet Grill

Kamado grills are very efficient, and bullet grills are more user-friendly for smoking than kettle grills. For either of these grills, you fill the basin with charcoal and wood chunks, light them, and dial the two vents (top and bottom) for a consistent temperature. One kamado cook can last twelve hours without having to replace any charcoal or wood chunks. Bullet grills are not as efficient but still burn nicely. A water pan isn't needed for kamado grills given how efficient and sealed they are, but bullets do benefit from one.

For the Offset Smoker

The offset is a firebox separate from the cooking chamber. A charcoal basket (literally a basket of charcoal) can be used to maintain the heat with wood chunks. Our preferred method is to start the offset with a healthy load of charcoal from a charcoal chimney starter and then add small log splits to the charcoal. As you continue to add logs as the fire burns down, the logs will burn into ember, keeping the heat component without needing more charcoal. The keys to using an offset are to make sure a flame is always burning in the firebox and to pay attention to the smoke color as a measure of success. Bad smoke is black (such as in a grease fire) or white (such as smothered fire.) Good smoke is light blue or barely visible smoke, meaning the fire has the most efficient combustion. Another important tip is to use warm wood. Place wood on top of the firebox to prewarm it; it will then burn faster when put into the firebox, preventing inefficient burning and producing a clean flame. This will result in the smoke flavor you are looking for. Water pans are great in an offset.

WINE

People love to tell you that BBQ and beer go hand in hand. It's that or whiskey. But what about the wine drinkers? Where do we fit in?

Some may suggest that most wines are far too delicate for BBQ or that BBQ is too intense and smoky for most wines.

Well, we call their bluff.

Any style of BBQ, whether traditional and regional styles or what we're doing here in the Pacific Northwest, has a wine that can pair. It's just about understanding a bit about how wine and food pairings work in general and applying that to any recipe cooked over a wood fire.

WHY WINE?

Well, there are some who can't imagine anything else but an ice-cold beer to drink with their spareribs, and that's absolutely fine. Go forth and enjoy that beer!

But there are others who want to know if it's OK to sip on merlot with those same ribs. And to those people we say, first, you don't need anyone's permission to drink wine with whatever the heck you're grilling or barbecuing, and, second, the answer is a resounding YES! Yes, you can!

This book is for you.

But if you're not a wine drinker at all, then this book is still for you! The wine, for those who love it, plays a minor yet important role. It's there to enhance and elevate the experience for those who choose it. But the recipes are the stars of this book, and wine is a supporting character. And of course, you don't need to drink anything to enjoy the seventy-plus recipes covered in this book. But if you happen to be wine curious and getting a little thirsty, read on.

Since this isn't a book about winemaking, our goal is to provide a basic understanding of how food and wine pairings work and how these principles apply to the wood-fired recipes in this cookbook. There are plenty of excellent resources if you would like to go into more depth about the wine-making process.

THE MYTH OF THE "PERFECT PAIRING"

We want to start off by saying that there is no such thing as a "perfect pairing." To imply something is perfect means it cannot be topped, it is without fault, unequivocal, flawless. That is impossible to achieve with something as subjective as taste.

No two people taste things exactly the same, so what may be perfect to me may not be perfect to you. We can go on and on about how amazing this lamb dish is with this bottle of pinot noir, but if you're just not a pinot noir fan, the pairing won't work for you and there is nothing we can do to convince you otherwise. Period. There's nothing wrong with the pairing; it's just not for you. And that's OK!

THE "RULES" OF FOOD AND WINE PAIRING

When you read about food and wine pairing, you're also likely to run into a series of rules, like "pair red wine with red meat," or "pair white wine with white meat and fish." While an adequate start, this is grossly oversimplified.

You might also learn that the number one "rule" of food and wine pairing is to "ignore the rules and drink what you like." While this is absolutely true (it is certainly important that you enjoy the wine in your glass), we do believe that there are some basic factors that can give you a base to understand an intricate subject without overthinking or oversimplifying it.

Wine is meant to be fun and enjoyable, not intimidating or rigid. So let's flush out the idea that there are any official rules to pairing wine with food. Instead, let's talk in terms of recommendations that will help you get the most out of any dining experience where wine is involved. Recommendations are just that, suggestions you can choose to follow or not. Who knows, maybe you'll even have an "aha" moment with a pairing that may just be perfect for *you*.

CREATING SYNERGY: As the great wine educators Kevin Zraly and Andrea Robinson suggest in Zraly's famous *Windows on the World Complete Wine Course*, the primary focus of any food and wine pairing should be about synergy—creating something that tastes better than the individual components do on their own (that "aha" moment referred to earlier).

It is also about balance. The food should not overpower the wine, nor should the wine overpower the food.

Pay attention to the following elements of food and wine, especially in how they apply to wood-fired cuisine.

COMPLEMENTING FLAVORS: The taste of the food and the wine being consumed together should be similar. Sauce shouldn't be sweeter than the wine, and the acid in the dish should be sufficiently matched to the acid levels in the wine. Now when it comes to the BBQ sauces in this book, most are certainly sweeter than any given wine recommended. But you'll apply the sauces sparingly or in a way that brings out the protein's flavor so that the BBQ sauce is not the dominant flavor. You'll have plenty of wine options with BBQ. More on this later.

CONTRASTING FLAVORS: Opposites attract. Match up contrasting flavors such as a sweet wine with a salty dish, a sweet wine with a spicy dish, or even a light, high-acid wine with a rich, fatty dish. This applies to many recipes in this book, where we tame a slightly spicy dish with a slightly sweet-style wine, creating synergy.

BODY AND WEIGHT: The weight of a dish should be matched by the weight of the wine.

When it comes to detecting the weight in wine, the best analogy we've heard is to compare skim milk with whole milk and heavy cream. Skim milk is light on the palate. The more you move toward cream, the heavier it feels on your palate. Light-bodied wines, like pinot gris, for example, feel more like skim milk, whereas full-bodied wines, like syrah or zinfandel, are closer to that whole-milk feel. Both white wines and red can fit into both light-bodied and full-bodied categories.

Oak usage in wine will generally translate to a heavier feel on your palate. Some wines say on the label if they have been aged in oak. Others won't. If you are unsure, it's best to ask the wine steward in your wine shop or liquor store.

FULL-BODIED DISHES WITH FULL-BODIED WINES: Our Wine-Braised Smoked Lamb Shanks (page 168) pair well with a full-bodied red wine like cabernet franc or a full-bodied syrah. Avoid pairing rich braised dishes like this with, say, a lighter-bodied pinot noir or gamay, since most are delicate and would be overpowered by a heavy, rich dish.

MEDIUM-BODIED DISHES WITH MEDIUM-BODIED WINES: Pair a dish like Smoked Whole Chicken (page 92) with a medium-bodied white wine or pinot noir. Avoid a heavy red wine because the light flavors of the dish would be overwhelmed.

LIGHT-BODIED DISHES WITH LIGHT-BODIED WINES: Pair a dish like Grilled Whole Trout (page 181), with an albariño or chenin blanc. As with the medium-bodied example above, a heavy wine would overpower a light, delicate dish.

FUNDAMENTAL ELEMENTS OF WINE AND FOOD PAIRING

ACIDITY: Acid is one of the most important factors to consider, and it is found in both food and wine. It's what keeps a wine lively on the palate and gives it an innate ability to pair with food because it acts as a palate cleanser. Good acidity in wine can be detected by a sharpness or jolt in the mouth, usually near the front of your tongue, followed by your mouth starting to water. In general, the more your mouth waters, the higher the acidity.

When it comes to pairing, the acidity of the dish should be matched by the acidity in the wine. This can be hard to detect, we know.

If the food is more acidic than the wine, then the wine will taste flabby or flat. Think about what happens to soda when the carbonation wears off; it gets flat, uninteresting, and all you taste is the sugar. Want to test this out? Try tasting a salad with lemon- and vinegar-based dressing (two ingredients that are very high in acidity) paired with a viognier or an oaked chardonnay from a warmer region in California. The wine, which has much less acidity than the dressing, will taste unbalanced and flat paired with the high-acid dish, but a high-acid wine, like sauvignon blanc, can work quite well.

Consider the pairing of Chianti (an Italian region and high-acid wine made from sangiovese grapes) and spaghetti or pizza (made with tomato sauce). The tomatoes are high in acid and the sauce is usually medium to heavy bodied. Both go well with a wine that is matched in weight and also high in acid. You'll find a similar pairing on page 125 with our Smoked Beef Lasagne, paired with sangiovese or barbera.

Generally speaking, wines from cooler climates tend to display higher levels of acidity. Wines high in acid include (but are not limited to) sparkling wine, sauvignon blanc, riesling, albariño, pinot gris/grigio, sangiovese, barbera, gamay, and pinot noir.

We're so passionate about Oregon wines because the majority of them are made in a cool climate, making them good candidates for food pairing, even BBQ.

ACIDITY IN BBQ: Similarly, acid pops up in BBQ in the form of sauces that have an apple cider base, as well as in condiments such as mustard and relish.

Take the Grilled Lamb Steaks with Salsa Verde on page 162, for example. The meat alone is a touch gamy and rich, but the green salsa topping the steaks is bright, herbaceous, and full of lively acidic flavors from the fresh lemon juice and apple cider vinegar. Acid is just as important in balancing out a dish, even BBQ, as it is in balancing out a wine.

SWEETNESS: Sweet is residual sugar, or sugar that is left after fermentation, that remains in the wine. Quite often it is confused for fruity characteristics that may have zero residual sugar. Lots of fruit aromatics can come across as "sweet," even though a wine could be technically "dry."

The golden rule of sweet foods and wine is that sweetness of a dish should be matched or exceeded by the sweetness of the wine (a dry wine would taste sour and unpleasant). When it comes to pairing sweet, understand that sweetness reduces perception of sweetness. When you taste a sweet wine paired with an equally sweet dish, you notice the perceived sweetness less. When paired correctly, they balance each other out, creating harmony.

This can be hard to detect (especially in desserts, which is why pairing wine and chocolate can be tricky but not impossible). Sweet wines also pair well with contrasting flavors, like spicy food. This is because sweet wines can help to cool and refresh the palate after a bite of something with a spicy kick to it. An example of a wine that can be sweet is riesling. More and more riesling wines now have a useful scale on the back of the label letting you know the sweetness level of the wine.

If a wine is described as "dry," then it usually has zero to very little residual sugar (or sweetness) to it.

SWEETNESS IN BBQ: Much of what has been written about BBQ and wine pairing implies that all BBQ is sweet (or heavy on the smoke), but this is simply not the case with the recipes in this book. While we have many sweet sauces, we hope that you'll find they are balanced out with a slight spice, that kiss of smoke, all balanced with the savory proteins they are applied to.

Don't be afraid of the seemingly sweet-looking recipes in this book. Our dishes are intended to be a balance of sweet, spicy, and savory. And like a well-made wine, not one element should dominate or stand out too much.

WINE COMPONENTS THAT INTERACT WITH YOUR MEAL

ALCOHOL: Alcohol is the result of fermentation, which is the biological process that converts sugars (naturally found in grapes) into energy, producing ethanol (alcohol) and carbon dioxide as by-products. The amount of alcohol in wine is based on various factors, such as how much sugar the grapes had to begin with before fermentation. Alcohol in wine ranges from around 9 percent alcohol by volume (ABV) on the very low side to 15 percent on the high side, with the majority of wines in the 12 percent to 14 percent range.

When it comes to pairing food with alcohol, consider the following: alcohol accentuates heat. Try tasting a high-alcohol wine like a zinfandel, which has more than 15 percent ABV, paired with a really spicy dish. Everything, both the wine and the dish, will taste hotter (the food will seem spicier and the wine will seem more alcoholic). For spicy dishes, it's best to serve a medium- to low-alcohol wine, or, for contrast, a wine that is slightly sweet and refreshing to cool and cleanse the palate. This is why beer and hot wings are a match made in heaven. But of course, this book isn't about beer.

Alcohol is accentuated by salt and pepper. This is important to consider with dry rubs, which can be both salty and sweet. Too much salt in a dish will make a wine seem "hot," or more alcoholic.

COOKING METHODS: Cooking methods, from sauté versus grilling versus smoking, will alter the flavor of any given food and its resulting wine pairing. The two styles of cooking provided throughout this book are grilling and smoking (as explained in Fire, page 9).

COOKING WITH WINE: Simply put, when cooking with wine, make sure you would willingly drink the wine you are cooking with. From there you can use almost anything. White acidic wines are great in a sauté, beurre blanc, or risotto. Reds can richen a marinade, be used for braising, or add flavor to a red sauce.

MARINATING: Marinating provides great complexity of flavor, while also tenderizing the meat. If wine is used as a part of the marinade, the acid in the wine will help break down the tough fibers of the meat. Marinating with wine is great for breaking down beef cuts like hanger or flank.

OAK IN WINE: Most red wines and some white wines (many chardonnays, in particular) are fermented and/or aged in oak barrels, often imparting subtle vanilla, caramel, oak, toast, char, or smoky characteristics to the wines. As mentioned above, oak can also impart tannins to wines. While oak can be a distracting factor in pairing with some cuisines, the flavors that result from oak can be quite complementary to grilled and smoked foods.

SAUCES: Sauces change all the so-called rules and will ultimately determine the wine recommendations. Sauces range from salsas or relishes to dressings to tomato-based sauces (like Kansas City–inspired sauces) to finishing glazes (like honey and a jam combined).

Take pork, for example. The Grilled Pork Chops with Dried Cherry Relish (page 157) leans toward red wine because of the flavors in the relish. But the Grilled Pork Tenderloin Medallions with Savory Apple Bacon Chutney (page 155) is better with a white wine. Same protein, different sauces, different wine-pairing potential.

TANNIN: Tannin in wine comes from two different sources: the skins and seeds of the grapes and the wood tannins that come from oak-barrel aging. Tannins are most commonly found in red wines (though they can be detected in whites as well).

Tannin is best described as the sensation it leaves in your mouth, which can be bitter and dry, astringent, and gritty. Picture unsweetened tea that has been steeped too long. The dry, gritty feeling that overcomes your tongue is tannin. Tannins tend to soften and mellow out with age. When it comes to pairing wines high in tannin with food, here are a few things to consider.

Fat and protein reduce the perception of tannin. This is why red meat and young cabernet sauvignon go so well together. The protein and fat from the beef soften the mouth-drying tannins from the wine.

Salt also reduces the perception of tannin. Try melting salty blue cheese on a grilled steak and pairing it with a cabernet sauvignon or a tempranillo from Spain's Rioja or Ribera del Duero regions. That element also reduces the otherwise noticeable tannins of the wine. It's also just a delicious combination!

THE WINES AND STYLES CHOSEN FOR THIS BOOK

There are thousands of grape varieties that have been used to make wine. Jancis Robinson, one of the world's renowned wine writers, wrote a book detailing 1,368 of them! And around 150 of those are commercially produced throughout the world.

"VARIETY" VERSUS "VARIETAL"

- **VARIETY** refers to a specific type of grape, like merlot or chardonnay.

- **VARIETAL** is a wine produced from a grape variety. In most New World countries, you'll see wines labeled by the name of the dominant grape in the bottle, such as cabernet sauvignon, zinfandel, or chardonnay. In Old World countries, you'll often see wines labeled by region, such as Bordeaux or Bourgogne.

For the purpose of this book, the grapes we have chosen to pair with these recipes are considered classic, international, or noble (noble grapes are grape varieties that are traditionally associated with the highest quality wines produced). They are grapes that have become household names and have international recognition and widespread consumer appeal. These are grapes that are widely planted and those you're likely to encounter at most wine shops or supermarkets.

We also reference some popular regional wines and blends (like Rioja, Bordeaux, and Côtes du Rhône) because, although they may not be single-varietal wines, they are great for some of the dishes recommended here and worth seeking out. They are distinct from their counterparts in other parts of the world (tempranillo grown in the Rioja region of Spain is distinctly different from tempranillo grown in Oregon, for example). So there are times when we specify which region is best for a certain dish.

You can't have a book about cuisine that is most popular during the summer months without mention of rosé, the quintessential summer drink. And since sparkling wine is our all-time favorite style of wine, it most certainly plays a central pairing role here as well.

Specific producers and vintages are not mentioned, but rather general regions, varietals, and styles that would pair with the recipes in this book.

It's also important to understand that the same grapes grown in different parts of the world can be vastly different. Heck, grapes grown in the exact same region, one mile apart, can taste vastly different. So if we recommend a sauvignon blanc for a dish, understand it will taste different if you open one from New Zealand versus the Loire region of France or California. The recommendations are meant to be a base. These are general guidelines. There will always be exceptions to every rule, every grape, every region.

And while we live in the Pacific Northwest (PNW) and are surrounded by incredible wines and diversity of regions, we won't limit the pairings exclusively to those produced in the PNW (though they will be predominantly showcased throughout the book). There is a world of great wine out there, and we encourage you to explore it. A good wine shop can be an invaluable resource to finding the right bottles to pair with the recipes in this book.

Food and wine pairing is a different experience for everyone. These pairings may not always work based on your personal preferences. But hopefully you'll develop the tools to understand what the recipe elements are and how they may react to your potential wines. You can then make adjustments to the food, based on your pairing.

Now let's get the party started!

WINE CHARACTERISTICS

WHITE WINES

VARIETY/VARIETAL	BODY	CHARACTERISTICS
Albariño	Light to medium bodied	Zesty, citrus, grapefruit, apricot, honeydew, pear
Arneis	Light to medium bodied	Dry, floral, fruity, peach, apple, honey, apricot, nuts
Chardonnay	Medium to full bodied	Wide range from crisp to full bodied, buttery, and creamy; range of apple, pear, citrus, pineapple, vanilla, caramel
Chenin blanc	Light bodied	Dry to off-dry, apple, lemon, pear
Gewürztraminer	Medium bodied	Dry to sweet, fragrant and floral, lychee, apricot, pear, baking spice
Grüner veltliner	Medium bodied	Herbaceous, apple, peach, citrus, minerals, white pepper
Pinot blanc	Medium bodied	Green apple, citrus, herbal, spicy, crisp
Pinot gris/grigio	Light bodied	Crisp and fruity, pear, peach, apricot, apple, citrus, melon
Riesling	Light bodied	Range from crisp and dry to sweet; apricot, apple, lemon, peach, nectarine, honeysuckle
Rosé	Light to medium bodied	Crisp and fruity, red berry fruit and citrus
Sauvignon blanc	Light bodied	Herbaceous, grassy, citrus, grapefruit, pineapple, peach
Sparkling	Light bodied	Crisp, apple, pear, bread, yeast
Torrontés	Medium bodied	Dry and aromatic, lemon, peach, flowers/rose petals
Viognier	Full bodied	Floral, apricot, pear, peach, honeysuckle, fruity, creamy

RED WINES

VARIETY/VARIETAL	BODY	CHARACTERISTICS
Barbera	Medium bodied	Fruity, red berry, plum, dark cherry, high acid
Cabernet franc	Medium to full bodied	Plum, strawberry, black cherry, roasted bell pepper, pepper, herbaceous
Cabernet sauvignon	Full bodied	Black currant, black cherry, blueberry, cassis, eucalyptus, oak, baking spice
Carménère	Medium bodied	Green bell pepper, plum, raspberry, cherry, blackberry, spice, dark cocoa, leather
Gamay	Light bodied	Bright, floral, fruity, raspberry, violet, black currant, tart cherry
Grenache	Medium bodied	Wide range based on region; strawberry, raspberry, black cherry, tobacco, white pepper
Malbec	Medium to full bodied	Dry and plump, dark fruit, smoky, black cherry, plum, raspberry, blackberry
Merlot	Medium to full bodied	Blackberry, plum, chocolate, vanilla
Mourvèdre	Full bodied	Dark color, dry, rich, spicy, plum, blackberry, blueberry, black pepper, violet
Petite sirah	Full bodied	Big, powerful, tannic, and dense; plum, blueberry, chocolate, black pepper, blackberry, licorice, spice
Pinot noir	Light to medium bodied	Range from fruity to earthy; cherry, cranberry, strawberry, rose, rhubarb, mushroom (earth)
Sangiovese	Light to medium bodied	Cherry, spice, fruity, acidic
Syrah	Full bodied	Ground pepper, spice, blackberry, blueberry, plum, violet, meaty
Tempranillo	Full bodied	Can be dry and big with high tannins and acidity; cherry, plum, tobacco, fig, vanilla, leather
Zinfandel	Full bodied	Plum, jam, blackberry, black cherry, tobacco

Regions or blends mentioned in this book: Beaujolais, Bordeaux and blends, Chianti, Rhône style (whites and reds), Rioja, Ribera del Duero

THE CHICKEN OF WINE: THE WIDE WORLD OF CHARDONNAY

A winemaker once told us chardonnay is the chicken of wine. It's a blank canvas. It takes on the flavors of where it's grown (all over the world, both in cool and warm climates) and how it's fermented (in a stainless-steel tank or in oak barrels). You can season it simply or go full throttle and let it age in a new oak barrel, imparting strong flavors. It's a chameleon that changes in style from light and fruity to lean and austere to acidic to full bodied and rich, all depending on where it's grown and how the winemaker chooses to express the grapes. For the chardonnay recommendations in this book, a note of style is included: aged in oak, unoaked, or specified by region (chardonnay from Chablis, for example, is minerally and austere, whereas chardonnay from California is fruity and rich).

A PINK PARTY: WHAT TO KNOW ABOUT ROSÉ

Rosé wines are generally produced from red grapes. When grapes are pressed (before fermentation), the juice of nearly every single grape runs clear. The skins give wine its color. With red wines, the grapes are pressed and ferment with their skins attached. With white wines, the skins are removed before fermentation, leaving that pure juice and clear color. With rosé, one method of achieving this is through maceration. In this method of production, red grapes are pressed and can spend up to twenty-four hours soaking in the skins, imparting some color before the juice is separated from the skins.

Saignée, or "bleeding," is another method whereby, similar to the process above, the grapes sit in their skins, allowing some the juice to "bleed" off into a new vat to produce a rosé. What remains of the red will be more concentrated and intense.

In some cases, rosé can be made by blending finished red and white wines together (this is common with rosé sparkling wine), but the best examples are produced using the maceration method above.

Rosé wines range from light, crisp, and bright to dark, intense, and deeply fruity. You may also see some labeled blush or white zinfandel, and these can be intensely sweet. The wines recommended in this book lean toward the dry style, as we find them more refreshing and better suited to our recipes.

LET'S GET BUBBLY

Champagne is truly Mary's favorite beverage in the world. But let's be clear on one thing: true Champagne only comes from the Champagne region of northeast France. The word Champagne has become synonymous with all things sparkling wine. But there's a big difference between the sparkling wine produced in this region of France and those produced elsewhere.

So what is Champagne then?

Champagne is produced by a process referred to as *méthode traditionnelle* (or *méthode champenoise*), when, after primary fermentation (the fermentation that converts sugar to alcohol), the wines go through a secondary fermentation in the bottle. The then-still wine is placed into a bottle, along with a small amount of yeast and sugar to initiate the second fermentation. This creates carbon dioxide, which in turn forms the bubbles, or effervescence, once the bottle is opened.

There is sparkling wine produced throughout the world in this same method, but only true Champagne comes from the Champagne region of France, where the wines are incredibly distinct from those made elsewhere.

Even within France, but outside of the Champagne region, you'll find sparkling wines labeled Crémant, such as Crémant de Bourgogne (sparkling wines from Burgundy), Crémant de Loire (sparkling wines from the Loire region), and so forth. These are made using the *méthode traditionnelle* and can be quite delicious, but they are not Champagne.

In Spain you'll find fruity and crisp sparkling wines labeled as Cava. These can be great values. Prosecco sparkling wines from Italy are produced in the Charmat method, where the bubbles are typically produced inside a large pressurized tank (versus inside the bottle).

Elsewhere, sparkling wines are commonly made by using the *méthode traditionnelle* throughout the world. A small number of wine producers are also carbonating the wines, which can help to keep costs down, but the quality of the bubbles are often sacrificed.

Sparkling wines are fantastic food-pairing wines and are recommended throughout the book. These wines aren't just for celebrations or aperitifs. These can and should be dinner wines as well, and we hope you're motivated to try some with your next whole smoked chicken.

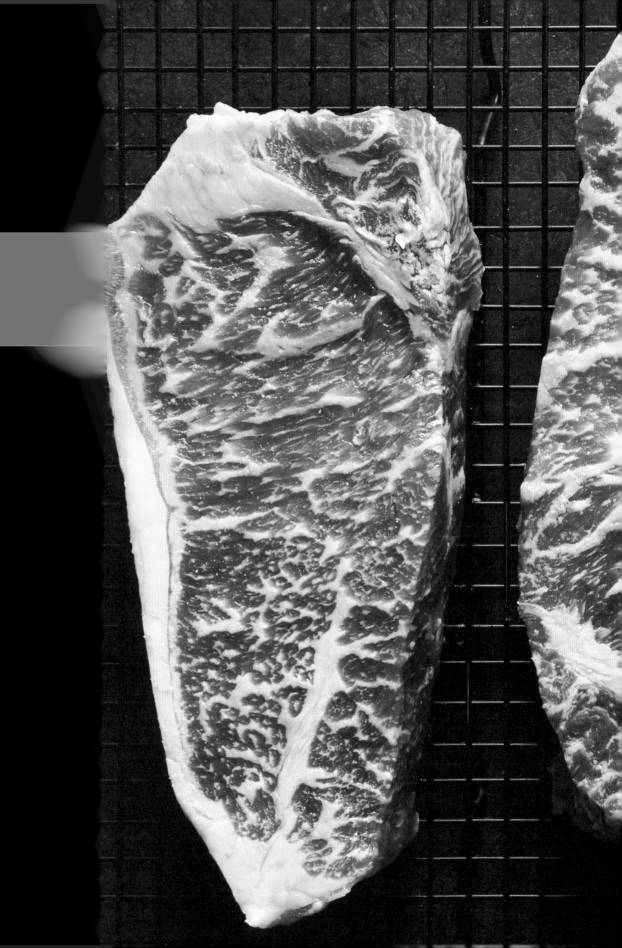

RECIPES

RUBS, SAUCES, AND GLAZES

Before, during, and after the cooking process, the addition of other flavors can really elevate your food. Rubs can bring sweet or salty elements, which in turn can contrast with or complement your protein. A great example is a rich, buttery cut of whitefish. Adding a salty and savory rub will contrast with the natural sweetness and bring out added flavor.

Our approach is to allow the authenticity and simplicity of flavors to shine. The addition of a rub or condiment should simply enhance, not drown, what the underlying food really offers—much like our philosophy of smoke as an ingredient. The main star is always the protein, vegetable, or fruit that is being cooked over wood fire.

We also hope that you take these concepts and experiment to find your own favorite flavors. It's actually very easy to do.

Salt is a great example. No matter how much we love a certain ratio of salt, some people will feel we oversalt, and others will feel we don't use enough. The Goldilocks of salt comes down to your palate. Sure, there is a science to salt in brines as an example. That said, your journey through fire and wine comes down to what you like. So always feel free to adjust after you have tried these recipes and adapt them to your personal preferences.

SWEET RUB

This is a great all-purpose rub for pork and smoked poultry. It starts with a generous amount of brown sugar, which is balanced out with some savory and a hint of spice. Since this rub contains sugar, you won't want to use this with high-heat grilling because it runs the potential to burn. In high-heat scenarios, go with the Beef Rub or the Savory Rub (opposite page).

MAKES 1½ CUPS DRY RUB

1 cup dark brown sugar

¼ cup kosher salt

2 tablespoons smoked paprika

2 tablespoons coarse ground black pepper

1 tablespoon granulated garlic

½ teaspoon cayenne pepper

In a small bowl, combine all of the ingredients. Store in an airtight container for up to 6 months.

POULTRY RUB

A great all-purpose poultry rub, from chicken to turkey to duck, this also works well on some pork dishes, such as roasts. With a much lighter sugar quantity than the Sweet Rub (above), it tends to do well over direct heat in addition to smoking low.

MAKES 1½ CUPS DRY RUB

½ cup dark brown sugar

¼ cup kosher salt

¼ cup coarse ground black pepper

¼ cup paprika

2 tablespoons granulated garlic

1 tablespoon dried sage

1 tablespoon dried thyme

½ teaspoon dried cayenne pepper

In a small bowl, combine all of the ingredients. Store in an airtight container for up to 6 months.

BEEF RUB

For big and bold beef flavors, we like to keep it simple when seasoning the king of meats. This rub is also great for big, rich veggies like portobello mushrooms.

MAKES 2 CUPS DRY RUB

⅔ cup kosher salt

⅔ cup coarse ground pepper

⅔ cup granulated garlic

2 teaspoons paprika

1 teaspoon cayenne pepper

In a small bowl, combine all of the ingredients. Store in an airtight container for up to 6 months.

SAVORY RUB

This is our go-to rub for a lot of direct grilling. With no sugar and a slight herbal finish, it is great for grilling fish, veggies, game meat, and lamb.

MAKES JUST OVER 2 CUPS DRY RUB

1 cup kosher salt

⅓ cup paprika

⅓ cup coarse black pepper

⅓ cup granulated garlic

2 tablespoons dried rosemary, ground in a pestle or crushed by hand

2 teaspoons ground thyme

1 teaspoon cayenne pepper

In a small bowl, combine all of the ingredients. Store in an airtight container for up to 6 months.

HONEY GOLD SAUCE

Our Honey Gold Sauce is influenced by the Carolinas. The spicy vinegar flavor and Dijon tang complement most pork and fish recipes with the slight sweet added by the honey and sugar.

MAKES 2⅔ CUPS SAUCE

2 cups apple cider vinegar

⅓ cup Dijon mustard

¼ cup hot sauce

¼ cup dark brown sugar

¼ cup honey

1 tablespoon whole peppercorns

1½ teaspoons kosher salt

In a medium saucepan over medium heat, combine all of the ingredients. While stirring, bring to a simmer, about 1 to 2 minutes, then reduce the heat to low. Continue cooking at a low simmer, stirring slowly, for another 20 minutes. Remove from the heat and strain the liquid. Allow to cool, discard the solids, and pour into an airtight jar. Refrigerate overnight. Shake before using. The sauce will keep in the refrigerator for up to 3 months.

PINOT NOIR BBQ SAUCE

One of our first catering events took place at Phelps Creek Vineyards in Hood River, Oregon, for an annual summer wine club event. We made pulled pork sandwiches with an original BBQ sauce. Knowing that Phelps Creek wines are light and elegant, we didn't want a rich, sweet, or spicy BBQ sauce interfering with the delicate nature of its pinot noirs. A traditional Kansas City–style BBQ sauce full of sweet tomatoes and heat would have overpowered these beautiful wines. So we decided to use pinot noir in the sauce and decrease the intensity by limiting the bolder spices. It was such a hit that this sauce became our favorite for most Oregon winery events.

MAKES 1½ CUPS SAUCE

1 tablespoon olive oil

⅓ cup chopped shallots or red onion

2 cloves garlic, minced

1 tablespoon chili powder

½ teaspoon dry mustard

¼ teaspoon cayenne pepper

1 cup pinot noir or other light-bodied red wine such as gamay or grenache

1 cup ketchup

In a medium saucepan over medium heat, heat the oil and then add the shallots. Cook, stirring occasionally, until the shallots are translucent, about 5 minutes. Turn down the heat if you see browning. Add the garlic and cook for 2 minutes, stirring occasionally. Add the chili powder, mustard, and cayenne, and stir constantly for 1 minute.

Add the pinot noir and turn the heat to high. Bring the wine to a boil and then reduce the heat to simmer for 5 to 7 minutes, stirring occasionally until reduced by about one-fourth to one-third to concentrate the flavor. Add the ketchup and bring back to a simmer, stirring, for about 5 minutes. Remove from the heat, allow to cool, and pour into an airtight container. Refrigerate overnight. Shake before using. The sauce will keep in the refrigerator for several weeks. It will thicken when chilled. To thin it out, add 1 tablespoon water at a time and stir until the desired thickness.

Variation

The Pinot Noir BBQ Sauce is intended to be served with a mild wine. However, if you want more boldness and depth add these ingredients to your sauce for a more savory and hot variation.

MAKES ABOUT 2 CUPS SAUCE

2 tablespoons brown sugar

1 tablespoon Dijon mustard

1 tablespoon Worcestershire sauce

1 tablespoon apple cider vinegar

Just after adding the ketchup, add the brown sugar, Dijon, Worcestershire sauce, and vinegar. Bring to a simmer and cook for about 8 minutes, stirring frequently. Remove from the heat, allow to cool, and pour into an airtight container. Refrigerate overnight. Shake before using.

EASY CAROLINA-STYLE BBQ SAUCE

This is where Sean's allegiance to sauces began. The Carolinas have a great tangy vinegar sauce that is simply prepared and is terrific for dipping or mopping your meat. It has a peppery finish and a lot of acidity, and it actually pairs really well with wine. This is a great sauce to use on pork.

MAKES 2½ CUPS SAUCE

2 cups apple cider vinegar
½ cup ketchup
¼ cup hot sauce
¼ cup turbinado sugar

2 tablespoons whole black peppercorns
1 tablespoon red chili pepper flakes
1½ teaspoons kosher salt

In a medium saucepan over medium heat, combine all of the ingredients. While stirring, bring to a simmer, about 5 minutes, then reduce the heat to low. Continue cooking at a low simmer, stirring frequently, for another 15 minutes. Remove from the heat and strain the liquid. Allow to cool, discard the solids, and pour into an airtight jar. Refrigerate overnight. Shake before using. The sauce will keep in the refrigerator for up to 3 months.

What Is Our Regional Style?

We were influenced early on by the Carolinas and vinegar-based sauces. The acidity balances well with wine and adds great flavor to food. Living in the Pacific Northwest, we combine vinegar sauce with berries and fruits that are prevalent everywhere, including wild blackberries, blueberries, cherries, and apples. The fruit element can be fresh during the season, or we may add a jam component during the winter and early spring months. Plus, we add wine, because wine is also bountiful here.

We define sauces broadly to include any condiment added to meat. This can include aioli, mayonnaise, beurre blanc, relishes, and even dried additions like savory granola. Our philosophy is the meat is the star, and the sauce is along for the show, with the wine complementing both.

MERLOT WINE SPRITZ

A spritz is great for adding flavor to meats cooked low and slow. It's not as intense as a marinade, but it adds moisture to the cooking, as well as more depth of flavor.

MAKES 3½ CUPS SPRITZ

2 cups beef stock

1½ cups merlot or other full-bodied bold red wine

2 cloves garlic, chopped

2 tablespoons chopped shallots, or 1 small shallot

1 tablespoon whole black peppercorns

1½ teaspoons red chili pepper flakes

1 teaspoon kosher salt

In a medium saucepan over low to medium-low heat, combine all of the ingredients. Let simmer (but not come to a boil) for 30 minutes, uncovered. Do not simmer for more than 1 hour to avoid it reducing. Remove from the heat and strain the liquids. Discard the solids. Cool in the refrigerator.

Pour the spritz into a food-safe spray bottle. The spritz can be used right away or made the day before using. It will keep in the refrigerator for up to 1 week.

BOURBON CHIPOTLE CHERRY GLAZE

A glaze is a great way to finish any meat, generally applied just as cooking nears completion. This glaze brings sweet and savory with a touch of bourbon and is very versatile. You can use it on almost any protein, and it holds up to wine. The bourbon cooks down while still highlighting the caramel and bourbon characteristic. The chipotle pepper, from a small can of chipotle in adobo sauce, adds great smoke and heat to the sauce, which is balanced by the sweet cherry jam.

MAKES JUST OVER 2 CUPS GLAZE

1½ teaspoons olive oil

¼ cup finely diced red onion

2 cloves garlic, minced

1 cup ketchup

¼ cup apple cider vinegar

¼ cup bourbon

¼ cup cherry jam

1 tablespoon blackstrap molasses

1 tablespoon dark brown sugar

1 tablespoon chopped chipotle pepper in adobo

¼ teaspoon kosher salt

⅛ teaspoon cayenne pepper

In a medium saucepan over medium heat, heat the oil. Add the onions and sauté for 5 minutes, or until translucent but not caramelized. Reduce the heat if you see any browning. Add the garlic and cook for 1 minute until soft.

Add the ketchup, vinegar, bourbon, jam, molasses, brown sugar, chipotle, salt, and cayenne, and bring to a simmer for 10 minutes. Cover because it will splatter. Remove from the heat, allow to cool, then transfer to an airtight jar and refrigerate. It will keep for up to 1 week.

BASIC AIOLI

Mastering an aioli will serve you well in so many ways. Once you have the basics down, you can add whatever you want to flavor it. Try adding your favorite dry rub or, for some heat, cayenne or dried chipotle seasoning one teaspoon at a time. Or for something fun, fold in one tablespoon BBQ sauce.

We cook almost exclusively with olive oil, but for an aioli, 100 percent olive oil can be a bit too intense. So, we cut it in half by using a neutral oil like avocado or grapeseed (vegetable oil works fine too).

MAKES 1 CUP AIOLI

1 large clove garlic

¼ teaspoon plus ⅛ teaspoon kosher salt

1 egg yolk

1 tablespoon fresh squeezed lemon juice

1 teaspoon Dijon mustard

1 teaspoon white wine vinegar

½ cup avocado oil or other neutral-flavored oil

½ cup extra-virgin olive oil

¼ teaspoon cayenne pepper

Using a large knife, mince the garlic and ⅛ teaspoon of the salt into a paste.

In a medium bowl, combine the garlic paste, egg yolk, lemon juice, Dijon, and vinegar. Whisk quickly for at least 30 seconds. Combine the two kinds of oil, then very slowly add a small amount of the oil mixture to the garlic mixture while continuing to whisk vigorously. Gradually add the rest of the oil in a very slow and thin stream, whisking, until the aioli thickens. The whole process should take 4 to 5 minutes, and the end result should look pale yellow and thick. Stir in the remaining ¼ teaspoon of the salt, cayenne, and any additional dry seasonings of your preference.

Cover and chill in the refrigerator for up to 1 week.

Variation

To make the Avocado Aioli (for the Grilled Sausage Endive Cups, page 84), smash 1 ripe avocado in a separate bowl into a creamy consistency, then gently fold into one batch of aioli.

STARTING THE PARTY

We love to greet family and friends with a fun series of light bites and wine when they come over for a gathering. There is a method to our madness for weekend cookouts. We try to prepare as much as we can in advance, so the day of the party is as easy as possible.

Offering simply prepared finger foods that your guests can enjoy with wine is the best way to keep things stress-free. Naturally, everyone ends up in the kitchen for a dinner party or on the deck for a cookout. Setting up stations in different areas encourages people to move around.

We almost always add a cheese station along with our party nuts, smoked honey butter, and bread, and then place the food with the paired wine around the house or backyard. This way you can enjoy the bite and stage the appropriate wine next to the setup. This naturally allows everyone to pour a wine that fits that specific dish.

You are now free to simply restock what has already been prepared while you are cooking away for your main course.

GRILLED CEDAR PLANK BRIE AND STRAWBERRY BALSAMIC GLAZE

This ain't your typical baked brie smothered in jam. This one is cooked on a cedar plank over a wood fire, infusing it with sweet smoke, and topped with a rich berry balsamic glaze. Feel free to substitute other berries. Blueberries work well for a milder (less sweet) taste, while strawberries provide a bright, bold, sweet contrast to the balsamic and creamy cheese.

MAKES 1 BRIE WHEEL, OR 6 TO 8 SERVINGS

1 cup sliced strawberries

¼ cup balsamic vinegar

2 tablespoons brown sugar

1 tablespoon honey

¼ teaspoon kosher salt

1 (8-ounce) wheel brie cheese

Shaved smoked almonds, for garnish (optional)

Special tool

1 cedar plank

One hour before cooking, pour water into a large dish and submerge the cedar plank in it. You can cut your plank in half to accommodate the brie wheel. Save the other half for another day.

In a small saucepan over medium-low heat, combine the berries, vinegar, brown sugar, honey, and salt. Stir until it reaches a simmer, and continue to simmer for 15 minutes to thicken. Place in the refrigerator for 30 minutes to 1 hour to set into a jam-like consistency.

Prepare the grill for direct/indirect cooking, with a target temperature of 400 degrees F.

Remove the cedar plank from the water, and place the brie wheel directly on the plank. Top the brie with the berry glaze. Place over indirect heat, and cover the grill. Remove after 8 to 10 minutes, or until the cheese softens. Top with shaved almonds, and serve warm with your favorite crusty bread or crackers.

WINE PAIRING: We're just getting the party started here, so rosé (sparkling or still) would be our choice. A mildly oaked chardonnay works well too, depending on the berries you use, especially with the smoky tones from the cedar plank.

SMOKED SALMON CROSTINI WITH CAPERS, DILL, AND GOAT CHEESE

There are so many great uses for Northwest salmon. If you don't want to commit to a full meal but still want a salmon fix, this is a great appetizer for parties. We created this recipe for one of our favorite annual events at Anne Amie Vineyards called Counter Culture, a celebration of street food.

MAKES 24 CROSTINI

For the crostini
- 1 baguette, cut at a slight bias into 24 (¼-inch-thick) slices
- 2 tablespoons extra-virgin olive oil
- 2 cloves garlic, peeled

For the salmon
- ½ pound wild salmon, such as coho
- 1½ teaspoons good-quality Dijon mustard
- 1 teaspoon kosher salt
- 1 teaspoon coarse ground black pepper

For the topping
- ⅓ cup plus 1 tablespoon crème fraîche
- ⅓ cup goat cheese, room temperature
- 1 tablespoon chopped fresh dill
- 1 tablespoon freshly squeezed lemon juice
- 1½ teaspoons capers, chopped
- ¼ teaspoon lemon zest (from 1 lemon)
- ⅛ teaspoon kosher salt
- Finishing or Maldon salt

To make the crostini, preheat the oven to 375 degrees F. Place the baguette slices on a baking sheet. Using a silicone brush, lightly coat the tops of the slices with the oil. Bake for 12 minutes, or until the crostini are slightly golden. Remove the crostini from the oven, and rub them lightly with the garlic. The garlic will almost melt into the bread for added flavor. This can be done earlier in the day.

To smoke the salmon, preheat the smoker to 225 degrees F using cherrywood.

Using tweezers, remove any pin bones from the salmon. Coat the flesh with the Dijon and season with salt and pepper.

Place the salmon on the smoker for up to 1 hour, or until the internal temperature is 130 degrees F. Remove the salmon and shred it gently with your fingers, leaving some large chunks. This can be done in advance.

To make the topping, in a large bowl, combine the crème fraîche, goat cheese, dill, lemon juice, capers, lemon zest, and kosher salt. Place the mixture in a ziplock bag, cut a small corner off the bag, and pipe about 1½ teaspoons of the filling onto each crostini. Top with a few pieces of salmon and a touch of finishing salt.

WINE PAIRING: Though salmon and pinot noir are a classic pairing, this preparation lends itself quite well to a riesling, crisp chardonnay, and even sparkling wine.

SMOKED WHITE BEAN DIP

We probably overdid it on hummus a couple years ago because now we won't go near it. This smoked white bean dip is such a refreshing change. It is creamy and rich in texture but mild, bright, and fresh in flavor. This is our new house dip! Pair with crackers or vegetables for the perfect mid-day snack or party appetizer.

MAKES 1½ CUPS DIP

1 (15-ounce can) northern or white beans

¼ cup chopped red onion

2 tablespoons freshly squeezed lemon juice, plus more if needed

1 clove garlic, crushed

¼ teaspoon kosher salt

¼ teaspoon coarse ground black pepper

¼ teaspoon chopped fresh thyme

¼ cup extra-virgin olive oil, plus more if needed and for garnish

Flaky sea salt, for garnish

Preheat the smoker to 225 degrees F using applewood or any fruitwood.

In a small smoker-safe dish, add the beans, including the liquid.

Smoke for 3 hours (the liquid will start to evaporate and the beans will start to look dry). Stir the beans every 30 minutes; otherwise, only the beans on top will take on the smoke. Remove the beans from smoker.

In a food processor, combine the beans, onion, lemon juice, garlic, kosher salt, pepper, and thyme, and begin to pulse. Slowly pour in the oil, and continue to pulse, until the texture is smooth, almost like hummus. If the dip is too dry, add more oil or up to a tablespoon lemon juice as needed.

Place in a serving bowl, garnish with a drizzle of good-quality olive oil and a sprinkling of flaky sea salt to taste, and serve with crackers and vegetables.

WINE PAIRING: This dip works quite well with a fruity albariño from Spain or even an Italian pinot grigio. Their lemony richness is a great match for the brightness of the dip.

SMOKED BONE MARROW

Bone marrow can be intimidating to eat and even more intimidating to cook, but it's actually super easy to prepare and has some of the richest flavor of all the cow. Plus, it's full of incredible nutrients, and it makes an impressive appetizer for a dinner party. Serve one marrow bone per couple with crusty toasted bread. Watch as everyone devours the marrow and talks about how much they look forward to the next time they come back for more.

MAKES 6 TO 8 SERVINGS

3 pounds, or 4 canoes, bone marrow (see note)

½ teaspoon kosher salt

½ teaspoon coarse ground black pepper

4 teaspoons extra-virgin olive oil

1 loaf crusty bread, cut into ½- to ¾-inch-thick slices (we like Italian Como bread)

Preheat the smoker to 225 degrees F using applewood or cherrywood.

In a small bowl, combine the salt and pepper. Season each bone marrow with 1 teaspoon of the oil and top with the salt and pepper.

Place the bone marrow, marrow side up, on the smoker for 1 hour. The marrow will slightly liquify, and you will see some small bubbles coming out the sides. Don't smoke too long because you will lose some of the liquid (and this is liquid gold!).

When the marrow is nearly done, place the bread slices under the oven broiler for 1 to 2 minutes until toasted.

Remove the marrow from the smoker and serve immediately with the toasted bread. To do so, serve directly from the canoes, cut side up. Using the smallest spoon you can find, or a cheese knife, scoop out a small amount of the marrow and spread it on a piece of the toasted bread, as if you were slathering jam on toast.

NOTE: When buying bone marrow, you will need to find a specialty butcher. Often bone marrow is available frozen or must be special ordered. You want "canoes" of marrow bones for this dish, which means they are cut along the bone lengthwise.

WINE PAIRING: This delicacy is richly flavored yet maintains a deep elegance. Loire Valley cabernet franc (from Chinon) works if you're craving red. But we wholeheartedly think you should pair this rare treat with a nice Champagne (a blanc de blancs). You may be surprised how great of a match these two are.

$\longrightarrow$

Variation

Alternatively, you can grill the marrow. To do so, season the same way as on the previous page.

Then, over direct heat, sear the marrow side of the bone for 2 minutes, then flip and cook, marrow side up, an additional 8 to 10 minutes, or until the marrow is bubbling. Remove and serve immediately.

Add the sliced bread to the same grill over direct heat for no more than 1 minute per side to char.

Managing Space on the Grill to Make Room for Starters

Grill space is always a fun dance. Making sure your food is fully cooked, warm, and coming out when you want it can be a very time-consuming process. This is where it may be helpful to write down a timeline or prep sheet so you have a sequence of things ready and the fire warm and working when you need it. Consider all those things you can prep in advance, like your dips.

Reverse sear is a great way to have your meat smoked so you can simply finish over the grill. To keep your food warm or held at the right temperature, you can simply place the meat in a cooler (with no ice) and that will maintain an ambient temperature, keeping the meat "held."

The gradient method is also a helpful way to move your food around so the hot items can be placed over the coals close to the grill grate and you can keep other cuts warm on the indirect side.

SMOKED PORK TENDERLOIN CROSTINI

This became a popular appetizer for events we catered. You can really stretch a pork tenderloin by serving it in thin slices on baguette crostini and topping it with a sweet and creamy balance of BBQ sauce and crème fraîche. It makes for a delicious and elegant appetizer for parties, and it works well with leftover pulled pork too.

MAKES 32 CROSTINI

For the crostini
- 1 baguette, cut into 32 (¼-inch-thick) slices
- 2 tablespoons extra-virgin olive oil
- 1 large clove garlic, peeled

For the pork tenderloin
- 1 pork tenderloin, approximately 1¼ to 1½ pounds
- 2 tablespoons Sweet Rub (page 62)
- 1 tablespoon extra-virgin olive oil
- 1 cup (8 ounces) crème fraîche
- 2 teaspoons freshly squeezed lemon juice
- ½ teaspoon lemon zest
- ¼ cup Pinot Noir BBQ Sauce (page 66)
- ¼ cup chopped fresh parsley, for garnish

To make the crostini, preheat the oven to 375 degrees F. Place the baguette slices on a baking sheet. Using a silicone brush, lightly coat the tops of the slices with the oil. Bake for 12 minutes, or until the crostini are slightly golden.

Remove the crostini from the oven, and rub them lightly with the garlic clove. The garlic will almost melt into the bread for added flavor. This can be done earlier in the day.

To make the pork tenderloin, preheat the smoker to 225 degrees F using a fruitwood such as cherry.

Trim the silverskin off the tenderloin, and coat with the Sweet Rub and oil. Place on the smoker for 45 minutes to 1 hour, or until the internal temperature is 140 degrees F.

After removing the tenderloin from the smoker, let it rest for 10 minutes. Slice the tenderloin into paper-thin slivers.

In a medium bowl, combine the crème fraîche, lemon juice, and zest. Whisk to combine.

To construct the crostini, place two or three (depending on thickness) pieces of tenderloin on a slice of crostini, toasted side up. Add ½ teaspoon of the crème fraîche mixture, then ¼ teaspoon of the Pinot Noir BBQ Sauce. Garnish with parsley.

WINE PAIRING: The party is still young, so a young and fruity pinot noir or gamay feels right.

FIRE-ROASTED PEPPER QUESO DIP

Mary challenged Sean to see if they could come up with a meatless queso dip that would taste just as good. We went with a mix of peppers to provide earthy flavors, sweetness, and heat. The result is so good you may want to make a double batch. You won't miss the meat one bit. And this proves that you don't need Velveeta for a crowd-pleasing cheese dip!

MAKES 4 TO 6 SERVINGS

3 large Anaheim peppers

1 red bell pepper

1 jalapeño pepper

2 tablespoons butter

2 tablespoons all-purpose flour

1 cup whole milk

½ cup crème fraîche or sour cream

1 tablespoon Dijon mustard

1 cup shredded cheddar cheese

¼ teaspoon kosher salt

⅛ teaspoon freshly ground black pepper

Prepare the grill for direct grilling.

Place all the peppers over the direct heat. Rotate the peppers as the skin blackens, which can take a few minutes per side depending on the intensity of the heat. You want the skin to slightly char but not completely blacken or burn through the flesh of the pepper.

Remove from the heat, let cool enough to handle, then remove the skin. We like to run the pepper under cold water to help remove the skin. Dice the peppers and discard the seeds. The peppers can be prepared in advance of making the dip.

To make the dip, in a medium saucepan over medium heat, add the butter and flour. Whisk consistently to make a roux, about 3 minutes. If it bubbles or looks as if it is browning, reduce the heat.

Add the milk and bring to a simmer (not a boil). Stir for 3 minutes, or until it starts to thicken. Add the crème fraîche and Dijon, stirring for 1 minute. Add the roasted peppers, cheese, salt, and black pepper. Stir as the cheese melts. Remove from the heat.

Transfer the queso dip to a slow cooker or fondue pot and serve warm.

WINE PAIRING: If you're looking for something other than beer (which admittedly is great with queso), reach for something equally bubbly and refreshing. Prosecco or Cava work well.

GRILLED SAUSAGE ENDIVE CUPS WITH AVOCADO AIOLI

This is a great appetizer if you're looking for a light, meaty bite without the weight of bread for stability. Endive cups act as cute little sturdy boats for the sliced spicy sausage and creamy aioli and provide a nice crunchy contrast to the rich meat.

MAKES 30 TO 35 ENDIVE CUPS

Basic Aioli (page 69)

1 ripe avocado

¾ pound hot Italian sausage

3 endive lettuce pods, rinsed, dried, and separated (approximately 10 to 12 leaves per pod)

1½ tablespoons whole ground mustard

Prepare the Basic Aioli in a large bowl and set aside. In a small bowl, crush the avocado until creamy using a fork. Gently fold the avocado into the aioli. Transfer the avocado aioli to a ziplock bag and snip a corner to make a piping bag. Set aside.

Prepare the grill for direct cooking.

Place the sausages over direct heat, turning often and covering until the internal temperature is 160 degrees F, about 12 minutes. Remove from the heat. When cool enough to handle, cut into ¼-inch-thick slices at a slight angle. You should get 10 to 12 slices per standard-size sausage.

Construct the endive cups by adding a slice of sausage, 1 teaspoon aioli (piped out of the bag), and a small dollop of mustard (about ⅛ teaspoon).

WINE PAIRING: This is a shoo-in for a German riesling. The wine's fruitiness and acidity cut through the richness of that juicy meat gorgeously. You could also opt for pinot grigio or another bright, fruity white wine. But carefully consider riesling first.

GRILLED MIXED PEPPER SALSA VERDE

Grilling peppers adds an earthy and smoky element to any salsa or recipe using peppers. Inspired by a family history of salsa makers, we add the grilled peppers to a generations-old salsa, giving it an extra flavor kick.

MAKES 4 CUPS SALSA

4 to 5 Anaheim peppers (about ½ cup after grilled and chopped)

4 to 5 poblano peppers (about ½ cup after grilled and chopped)

2 serrano peppers (1½ teaspoons after grilled and chopped)

1 (15-ounce) can stewed tomatoes

6 green onions, cut into thirds

1 cup fresh cilantro

3 cloves garlic, crushed

2 tablespoons apple cider vinegar

1 tablespoon freshly squeezed lime juice

½ teaspoon kosher salt

Prepare the grill for direct cooking.

Place the peppers over direct heat for 3 to 4 minutes per side, or until charred. This can take up to 14 minutes. You just want to blacken the skin with slight bubbles; any further charring will scorch the peppers and it will taste burned.

Remove the peppers from the grill and let cool enough to handle. Peel off the skin and remove most of the seeds. Roughly chop the peppers and put them in a food processor.

In the food processor, add the tomatoes, onions, cilantro, garlic, vinegar, lime juice, and salt, and pulse until pureed. The texture should resemble a thick blender salsa.

Serve with chips.

WINE PAIRING: Inviting your friends over for a thought-provoking salsa and wine-pairing party isn't really a thing (though I'd be excited to attend if you should throw one). Most likely this is the prelude to a bigger event with a spread of diverse flavors. Nonetheless, if you're looking for something to go with your corn chips and those slightly spicy, earthy, and herbal flavors, a fruity rosé will never let you down. Remember, we're still just getting the party started!

WINE MARINATED BEEF SKEWERS WITH CHERRY-BOURBON GLAZE

This is one of our favorite appetizers to serve at events. We can prep everything in advance, skewer them up in unison, keep them in a cooler until it's time to grill, and then cook to order so they can be served hot and fresh. The savory marinade and intoxicating cherry BBQ sauce is quite an unexpected treat at the end.

MAKES 14 TO 16 INDIVIDUAL SKEWERS; 6 TO 8 SERVINGS AS AN APPETIZER OR 4 SERVINGS AS A MAIN COURSE

For the cherry-bourbon glaze
- 1½ teaspoons extra-virgin olive oil
- ¼ cup finely diced red onion
- 2 cloves garlic, minced
- 1 cup ketchup
- ¼ cup apple cider vinegar
- ¼ cup bourbon
- ¼ cup cherry jam
- 1 tablespoon blackstrap molasses
- 1 tablespoon dark brown sugar
- ¼ teaspoon kosher salt
- ⅛ teaspoon cayenne pepper

For the marinade
- 1 cup dry red wine
- ½ low-sodium beef broth
- ½ cup diced red onion
- 3 cloves garlic, crushed
- 2 sprigs fresh rosemary
- 8 stems fresh thyme

For the skewers
- 2 New York strip steaks (1½ pounds), cut into 1-inch cubes
- 1 (15-ounce) package cremini mushrooms
- 1 large red onion, sliced into large pieces
- 1 pint cherry tomatoes
- ¼ cup Beef Rub (page 63)

Special tools
- Immersion blender
- Small wooden skewers

One hour before cooking, soak the skewers (if wood) in water in a large dish or ziplock bag.

To make the glaze, in a medium saucepan over medium heat, heat the oil and then add the onion. Sauté for 5 to 7 minutes until the onions are softened but not caramelized. Add the garlic and cook for 1 minute.

Add the ketchup, vinegar, bourbon, jam, molasses, sugar, salt, and cayenne and bring to a simmer. This should take roughly 5 minutes. Using an immersion blender, blend the sauce to liquefy the onions and garlic, 1 to 2 minutes. Let the glaze simmer (but not boil) for another 10 minutes. Allow to cool and then store in the refrigerator. The glaze can be made in advance.

To make the marinade, in a 1-gallon ziplock bag, combine the wine, broth, onion, garlic, rosemary, and thyme.

$\longrightarrow$

To prepare the skewer items, remove the stems from the mushrooms, wipe them clean, and cut them in half or quarters based on the size of the mushroom. Place the steak, mushrooms, and onions in the bag of marinade. Marinate for at least 2 hours or overnight.

Prepare the grill for direct/indirect cooking. Remove the steak, mushrooms, and onions from the marinade and discard the marinade.

In a large bowl, add the steak, mushrooms, onions, and tomatoes. Sprinkle half of the dry rub into the bowl, and mix with your hands. Add the remaining dry rub and mix again to evenly coat.

Remove the wooden skewers from the water. To assemble the skewers, start with one tomato, then add one mushroom, one onion slice, and one steak cube. Use one of each item per small wood skewer for appetizer portions.

Place the skewers on the direct side of the grill, and grill for 3 to 4 minutes until you see grill marks. Flip, then grill for an additional 3 to 4 minutes until you see grill marks. Move the skewers to the indirect heat, apply the glaze liberally to both sides of the skewer, cover, and continue cooking until the steak reaches the desired internal temperature. We like to pull at 130 degrees F, or an additional 4 to 6 minutes on indirect heat (covered).

As soon as you pull the meat, glaze one last time. Let rest 5 minutes, or until the skewer is cool enough to handle. Enjoy as a bite.

WINE PAIRING: The char from the grilled steak, savory marinade, and sweet sauce make these excellent pairings for malbec, zinfandel, or even grenache. Stick with a fruity and bold red to stand up to the bold flavors of the meat and cherry glaze.

SMOKED PARTY NUTS

Our smoked almonds became so popular that we started providing them to wineries to sell in their tasting rooms. This version mixes three of our favorite kinds of nuts to cook on the smoker and incorporates our Sweet Rub (page 62), giving it a great balance of sweet and spice and everything nice. These make awesome holiday gifts (place in a small airtight jar with a cute handmade tag) and are great just to have on hand for a healthy midday snack in between meals. We love to bring a baggie of these with us in our carry-ons whenever we travel to fight the urge to buy airport snacks.

MAKES 6 CUPS NUTS

2 cups raw almonds

2 cups raw pecan halves

2 cups raw hazelnuts

3 tablespoons unsalted butter

2 tablespoons Sweet Rub (page 62), divided

Preheat the smoker to 225 degrees F using a fruitwood (apple) or nutwood (pecan). In a 3-quart ovenproof glass baking dish, add the almonds, pecans, and hazelnuts.

Smoke for 3 hours, tossing every hour. Remove the nuts and place them in a large bowl.

In a small saucepan over medium heat, heat the butter and 1 tablespoon of the Sweet Rub until the butter melts. Pour the butter and Sweet Rub mixture onto the nuts while the nuts are still hot and stir. Add the remaining 1 tablespoon Sweet Rub to the mixture and stir to combine.

Serve warm or let cool and store in an airtight container in your pantry for several weeks.

Party-Starter Wines

There is an art to sequencing wine during a party. When hosting a potluck or even a plated meal, we typically have a pattern to staging wines. It all starts with the arrival. Having sparkling wine on ice with the glasses laid out is a great way to have a versatile wine that will go with a variety of flavors. In addition to sparkling wine, high-acid wines are wonderful as they also pair well with a variety of foods. If you want a catering trick, sequence your apps in stations, with one specific wine placed at that station. That way, as your guests move around your event, they naturally pair the specific wine with the food. Then if you move into a main course, those wines are already laid out.

BIRDS ON THE BBQ

Chicken and BBQ go hand in hand, and there are several ways to prepare it that don't result in a dry, overcooked bird. The key is knowing when to pull it from the grill or smoker.

We also have an obsession with less common fowl. Game hens make a great individual meal for a dinner party, and you can cook them easily on the smallest of grills. Duck brings a rich flavor to any dish, much like sweeter beef. And of course, turkey, that traditional bird we have smoked for decades, gives us one of the best flavors we enjoy on Thanksgiving.

SMOKED WHOLE CHICKEN

This smoked whole roaster is a favorite Sunday meal for our family. Enjoy the shredded chicken leftovers for the remainder of the week, and use the remaining bones to make the most incredible Smoked Chicken Stock (page 94). You'll soon find out why this is one of the things we cook most often on the smoker.

MAKES 4 SERVINGS

1 (4- to 5-pound) whole roaster organic chicken

2 tablespoons extra-virgin olive oil

3 tablespoons Poultry Rub (page 62)

1 red onion, quartered

6 cloves garlic

1 lemon, quartered

The day before cooking, coat the chicken with the oil and Poultry Rub. Make a point to season inside the cavity as well. Cover and refrigerate until just before cooking.

Preheat the smoker to 225 degrees F using applewood or cherrywood.

Stuff the cavity of the chicken with the onion, garlic, and lemon. Place the chicken on the smoker for up to 90 minutes, or until the internal temperature in the thigh and breast is 165 degrees F. It is not uncommon for the thigh to come up to temperature faster than the breast. That is fine because the dark meat can hold the higher temperature for a little longer and still be juicy.

Let sit for 10 minutes, then slice and serve. Keep the bones for stock.

WINE PAIRING: To us, this is the quintessential dish for a full-bodied chardonnay. Chardonnay has creamy, slightly fruity, lemony, and oaky notes that mirror the chicken's mild smoky tones while having the body to match that flavorful meat. We recommend chardonnays from Oregon for their body and crisp acidity to cut through the richness of the tender chicken. Alternatively, you can reach for Rhône-style whites.

SMOKED CHICKEN STOCK

When smoking a whole chicken, don't discard the carcass. Use those infused bones to make the most incredibly flavorful stock. It freezes perfectly in quart-size containers and keeps in the freezer for months. Use in your favorite soups and stews to give them a lovely sweet kiss of smoke (even if you're not smoking meat for that particular soup, the smoked stock will give you the feeling you did).

MAKES 4 QUARTS STOCK

5 quarts water, plus more as needed during cooking

1 carcass from a 4- to 5-pound smoked organic chicken

3 stalks celery, cut into thirds

2 carrots, cut into thirds

1 onion, quartered

1 bunch fresh parsley (including stems or just stems if you used the leaves)

1 head garlic, unpeeled and cut in half crosswise

10 sprigs fresh thyme, or the equivalent of a small handful

1 tablespoon whole black peppercorns

2 bay leaves

In a large pot over high heat, place the water, chicken carcass, celery, carrots, onion, parsley, garlic, thyme, peppercorns, and bay leaves. The water should come high enough to just cover the chicken and veggies. Bring to a boil, then reduce to a simmer. Simmer for 4 hours covered, leaving a smidge of an opening.

Strain the contents through a fine colander (we like to strain twice—once to remove any large pieces and a second time through a very fine colander).

Chill the stock in the refrigerator overnight. The next day, remove any surface fat, then transfer the stock into quart-size containers. Use within a couple of days or freeze.

NOTE: You may find that the stock will get a bit gelatinous after it's chilled. That's OK (it's actually a good thing!). Once you rewarm it, the gelatinous texture will melt away. If it's too thick or rich for your liking, just thin it out with a bit of water. We also don't add salt on purpose so we can add salt as we use the stock for a dish.

GRILLED DUCK BREAST

Duck is such a wonderful cut to cook on the grill. A duck breast has an amazing fat layer with skin that renders and crisps up to give it a distinct flavor. With a beefy meat flavor versus a chicken flavor, this wine-friendly fowl melts in your mouth. It also makes for great conversation when your friends come over wondering what's on the grill. Don't let the simplicity of this recipe fool you; it is full of flavor. Make sure to buy your duck from a trusted source so you can cook it to a lower temperature, giving it better tenderness.

MAKES 4 SERVINGS

4 duck breasts

1 tablespoon extra-virgin olive oil

2 tablespoons Poultry Rub (page 62)

With a sharp knife, crosshatch the skin of the duck with two X marks. This will help with the rendering of the skin and flavor from the rub.

Season each duck breast with a light drizzle of oil and 1½ teaspoons of the Poultry Rub. Cover and refrigerate for at least 4 hours (up to 24 hours). Remove from the refrigerator 30 minutes before cooking.

Prepare the grill for direct/indirect cooking.

Place the duck, skin side down, over the direct heat, and cook for 3 to 4 minutes, or until a nice crust develops. Flip the duck over for 4 minutes, then move the duck to the indirect side of the grill. Cover and let cook for 4 to 6 minutes, or until the internal temperature is 140 degrees F. (While the recommended finishing temperature of poultry per USDA guidelines is 160 degrees F, we like our duck at a lower temperature, like beef, as we buy from sources we know provide quality meat.)

Remove from the grill, let sit for 5 minutes, then slice and serve.

WINE PAIRING: Pinot noir (New World and Old World), merlot, and even a young Rioja (crianza) work well.

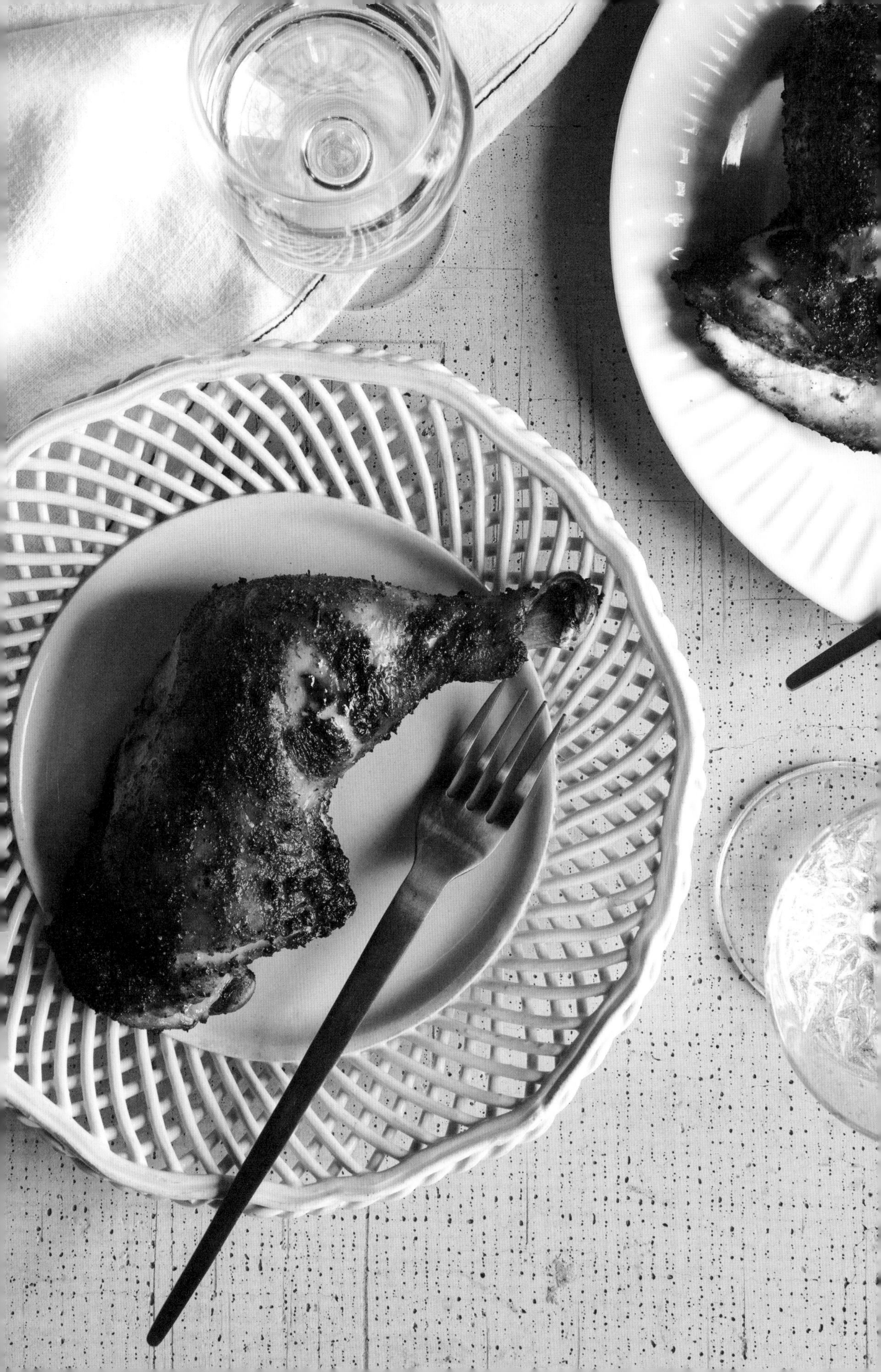

ROSEMARY BUTTERMILK GRILLED CHICKEN

Chicken is a flexible protein, happily adapting to any marinade, rub, sauce, or even cooking method. This highly flavorful chicken takes a long soak in a savory rosemary bath, allowing those flavors to seep in, serving to both flavor and tenderize the meat. When it's time to grill, the moisture is spot on and the taste is drool-worthy.

MAKES 6 SERVINGS

2 cups buttermilk

1½ teaspoons chopped fresh rosemary, divided

1 teaspoon kosher salt

1 teaspoon minced garlic

3 pounds chicken pieces, drumsticks and thighs, skin on

2 tablespoons Poultry Rub (page 62)

Prepare the buttermilk bath. In a 1-gallon ziplock bag, add the buttermilk, ¾ teaspoon of the rosemary, salt, and garlic. Add the chicken pieces to the bath. If the chicken thighs are large, you may have to split them between two bags. Marinate the chicken for 4 hours to 8 hours.

Remove the chicken from the bath and discard the marinade. Pat the chicken dry.

Prepare the dry rub in a small bowl by adding the remaining ¾ teaspoon of rosemary to the Poultry Rub. Season the chicken on both sides.

Prepare the grill for direct/indirect cooking.

Place the chicken over direct heat, paying attention to avoid flare-ups. Grill for 4 to 5 minutes, or until you have a nice crust. Then flip the chicken and grill the other side for 4 to 5 minutes.

Move the chicken to the indirect side of the grill and cover. Cook until the internal temperature of the chicken is 160 degrees F. Remove from the grill and let sit for 10 minutes before serving.

NOTE: If you marinate too long, the tenderizing element of the buttermilk can cause the skin to become rubbery.

WINE PAIRING: The meat is tender and full of savory flavors from that buttermilk bath with a nice crust from the grilling and a hint of herbs. Try this with a Chablis, viognier, grüner veltliner, or gewürztraminer to play with some of those herbal notes.

SMOKED AND GLAZED CHICKEN THIGHS

The flavor of smoked chicken is one of our favorites. But smoking chicken rarely results in crispy skin. There are certainly ways to achieve it, but you've got to get creative if you want both smoky and crispy. Similar to reverse searing a steak (page 21), the idea here is to smoke the thighs at a low temperature for flavor, then finish over direct heat for sear and to crisp up that flavorful skin. Adding the sauce toward the end allows it to flavor the skin without caramelizing or burning.

MAKES 4 SERVINGS (2 THIGHS PER SERVING)

8 chicken thighs (3 pounds)

2 tablespoons extra-virgin olive oil

2 tablespoons Sweet Rub (page 62)

1½ cups Pinot Noir BBQ Sauce (page 66) or your favorite Kansas City–style sauce

Trim the extra fat off of the chicken thighs. Coat the chicken with the oil and apply the Sweet Rub. This can be done the day before or up to 4 hours before cooking. Keep in the refrigerator until 30 minutes before cooking.

Preheat the smoker to 250 degrees F using cherrywood or applewood.

Place the chicken on the smoker and smoke until the internal temperature of the chicken is 155 degrees F, 45 to 60 minutes. Remove the chicken from smoker and brush on ¾ cup of the Pinot Noir BBQ Sauce. Prepare the smoker for direct cooking.

Place the chicken skin side down over direct heat for about 3 minutes. Keep the lid closed to avoid flare-ups. Flip the chicken and brush on the remaining ¾ cup Pinot Noir BBQ Sauce. Close the lid and cook 3 to 4 minutes, or until the sauce sets.

Remove the chicken from the grill and let sit for 10 minutes. Serve and enjoy right off the bone with your favorite sides and a glass of wine.

NOTE: If you are cooking on a pellet grill and don't have a direct grill feature, increase the temperature to the highest setting on your grill and place the chicken back on it for no more than 10 minutes, or until the internal temperature of the meat is 165 degrees F.

WINE PAIRING: We're looking for something on the bold side here. The chicken has a nice, rich smoke flavor and that sweet and savory BBQ sauce. This is where we like to reach for a zinfandel or a New World syrah (something with smoky, meaty notes works great).

GRILLED CORNISH GAME HENS

Game hens are a delightful treat for date night or to impress your friends. They have a similar flavor to chicken (yet are much smaller) with a slight sweet characteristic. Grilling game hens really enhances the flavors of this eclectic meat. These also make a great substitution for a whole turkey if you're doing Thanksgiving dinner for a small group (four or fewer people).

MAKES 4 SERVINGS (HALF A HEN PER SERVING)

2 whole game hens, roughly 2½ pounds each

2 tablespoons extra-virgin olive oil

2 tablespoons Beef Rub (page 63)

The day before serving, rinse and dry the game hens. Using a sharp knife, cut the hens in half so you have one side per serving as you season. Cut along the breastbone from top to bottom on both sides. Discard the breastbone or save for stock.

Coat the hens with the oil and liberally season with the Beef Rub, including the underside. Place the hens on a small baking sheet and put into the refrigerator, uncovered, for up to 24 hours. This will dry-brine and season the hens.

Remove hens from the refrigerator about 30 minutes before cooking. Prepare the grill for direct/indirect cooking.

Over direct heat, place the hens breast side down, and quickly sear for 3 to 4 minutes depending on how close the grates are to the charcoal (it could take up to 10 minutes depending on the heat source). The aim is for a nice sear as the milestone.

Flip the hens and move them to the indirect side. Cook for 10 to 15 minutes, or until the temperature in the breast and thigh are at least 160 degrees F using an instant-read thermometer.

Remove from the heat, let sit for 5 minutes, and enjoy.

WINE PAIRING: The simple preparation and quick grilling of these hens opens up to a wide range of pairing options. For white, try a chardonnay or viognier. For reds, a nice Beaujolais or a Côtes du Rhône or Rhône-style blend would work nicely.

How to Spatchcock a Bird

Lay a towel on your work surface and place a large cutting board on top of it to prevent the cutting board from slipping while you cut into the bird. Put on a pair of kitchen gloves.

Remove the giblets from the bird. Place the bird so the drumsticks are facing up on the cutting board.

Hold the bird firmly with one hand to keep it stable. Using a sharp knife, cut along the spine on both sides to remove the backbone. The backbone is not the side with the breasts. You may find that the bone is not cutting. If so, slowly move your knife to either side to work your way around the bone where there is a natural break. If you force the knife into the bone, you can chip the knife.

If you have a strong set of kitchen shears, it is easiest to lay the bird breast side down on the cutting board. Then holding the bird firm, cut along either side of the backbone. Good shears should cut right through the bone.

With the backbone is removed, place the bird breast side down and pull apart the cavity so you are pulling the sides away from each other. You will hear a cracking as the breastbone breaks. Flip the bird over so the breast side is facing up. Press down to flatten it.

Pat the bird dry and remove any bone fragments on either side before seasoning or brining.

Aren't you glad you wore the gloves?

Reserve the backbone for stock. Consider smoking or grilling it with your bird to add to the stock's flavor.

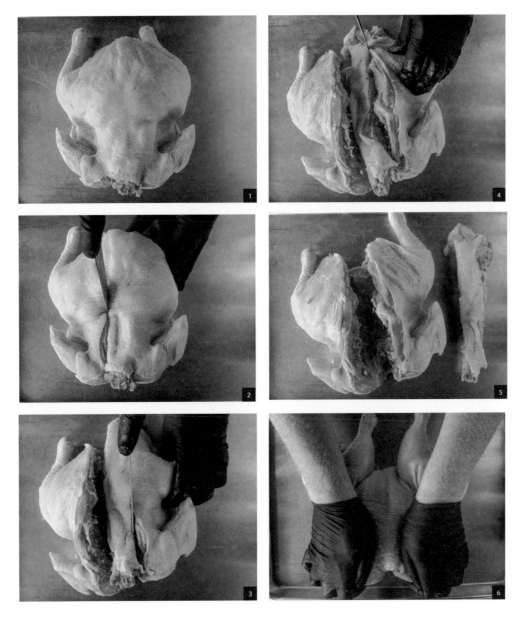

1. Place bird breast side down, neck facing away, backbone up top, and facing you.
2. Using a sharp knife or kitchen scissors, cut from the neck down, guiding knife along backbone.
3. Repeat the cut from step 2 along other side of backbone, toward you.
4. Finish the cut and set aside the backbone.
5. Pull each side away from each other to begin opening the cavity.
6. Flip the bird so that breast is now up, and press firmly down until the bird lies flat.

SPATCHCOCKED GRILLED CHICKEN

Unlike the Smoked Whole Chicken on page 92, this bird is spatchcocked (see page 102), which allows the whole chicken to cook on the grill at a high temperature without overcooking the legs and wings, while the breast meat and thighs come to temperature. Overcooked chicken is a sad, dry predicament. You can prevent that with this failproof technique.

MAKES 4 SERVINGS

1 (4- to 5-pound) roaster chicken

1 tablespoon kosher salt

1½ teaspoons coarse ground black pepper

1 teaspoon ground coriander

1 teaspoon marjoram

½ teaspoon dried sage

1 tablespoon extra-virgin olive oil

To spatchcock, using a sharp boning knife or strong kitchen shears, cut along the backbone of the chicken on both sides to remove it (you will cut both sides).

Flip the chicken so it is breast side up, and press down on the breastbone so you flatten out the chicken. Pat dry on both sides.

In a small bowl, mix together the salt, pepper, coriander, marjoram, and sage to form a dry rub.

Coat the chicken with the oil on both sides (1½ teaspoons per side) and then liberally apply the dry rub. Place on a baking sheet and put in the refrigerator for at least 4 hours, ideally overnight.

Prepare the grill for direct/indirect cooking.

Place the chicken over direct heat, breast side down, and cover. Sear for 5 to 8 minutes, watching out for flare-ups. Flip the chicken breast side up, cover, and cook for 10 minutes. Move the chicken to indirect heat and cook until the internal temperature is 160 degrees F in the breast and the thigh. This can take another 20 to 30 minutes.

WINE PAIRING: Chardonnay is a favorite with grilled chicken prepared like this. The crispy, well-seasoned grilled meat is a great match for a full-bodied chardonnay or other favorite full-bodied white. For red, reach for Beaujolais (gamay) or a light-bodied pinot noir. When in doubt, sparkling never disappoints with this meal.

How to Properly Take the Temperature of Poultry

1. Take the temperature in the thigh, taking care not to touch bone.
2. Take the temperature in the breast, taking care not to touch bone.
3. Check the thickest part of an individual breast.
4. Check the thigh, taking care not to touch bone.

SMOKED TURKEY DRUMSTICKS

At the first wedding we ever catered, the bride specifically wanted a turkey drumstick similar to the ones sold at Disneyland, one of their favorite places to go as a couple. In fact, the groom even proposed wearing a Mickey Mouse costume (too cute!), so this special dish had to be represented at the wedding. One of the key identifiers of those famous turkey legs are that they taste like ham, which is a result of a brine giving it a cured characteristic. In this version, we start with a twenty-four-hour brine, then coat it with a savory and sweet rub, giving it great flavor only enhanced by the smoking process. The end result was a very happy bride and groom on their wedding day and lots of photos with the giant turkey drumsticks!

MAKES 2 DRUMSTICKS

1 quart cold water	1 bay leaf
¼ cup kosher salt	2 (1-pound) turkey drumsticks, or the
¼ cup brown sugar	largest you can find
1 tablespoon black peppercorns	2 tablespoons extra-virgin olive oil
1½ teaspoons red chili pepper flakes	2 tablespoons Sweet Rub (page 62)

In a large bowl, pour in the water, then add the salt and brown sugar. Stir until the salt and sugar are dissolved. Add the peppercorns, pepper flakes, and bay leaf and stir again. Place the turkey drumsticks in a 1-gallon ziplock bag, then pour in the brining liquid. Brine for 10 to 24 hours.

Remove the drumsticks from the brining liquid, rinse with cold water, and pat dry with a paper towel.

Apply 1 tablespoon of the oil and 1 tablespoon of the Sweet Rub to each of the drumsticks.

Preheat the smoker to 275 degrees F. Place the drumsticks in the smoker for 90 minutes, or until the internal temperature is 165 degrees F. Let sit for 10 minutes and then enjoy! No forks required. But, of course, you can cut it off the bone for smaller portions.

WINE PAIRING: There are lots of options for this showstopper of a dish, such as a medium-bodied zinfandel, Oregon pinot noir, Beaujolais, Spanish garnacha, and deeply colored rosé (particularly from Spain). Choose your favorite and you can't go wrong.

SMOKED SPATCHCOCKED TURKEY

There's nothing like a perfectly cooked smoked turkey on Thanksgiving. The problem with a huge whole turkey is that those smaller pieces cook at different times, often leaving the wings or legs overcooked while the breast and thighs come to temperature. Spatchcocking is a fantastic way to get a more even cook for all parts of the bird. It's not your typical table-side presentation for the holiday bird, but it still makes for a dramatic look. The best part is that it has incredible flavor and everything is cooked to perfection.

MAKES 8 TO 10 SERVINGS

For the turkey

1 (12- to 14-pound) unbrined turkey

¼ cup extra-virgin olive oil

½ cup Poultry Rub (see page 62)

For the brine

8 quarts water

3 cups apple juice

1½ cups kosher salt

2 apples, quartered

1 white onion, quartered

½ cup honey

½ cup dark brown sugar

3 tablespoons black peppercorns

1 tablespoon red chili pepper flakes

2 bay leaves

To prepare the turkey, spatchcock it following the instructions on page 102.

To prepare the brine: 24 hours in advance, in a large stockpot, add the water, apple juice, salt, apples, onion, honey, sugar, peppercorns, pepper flakes, and bay leaves. Stir to combine. Add the turkey to the brine.

Place the stockpot in the refrigerator until ready to cook. If your refrigerator is not big enough, then place it in a large cooler with ice. You could also transfer the contents to a large brine bag and place it inside a cooler with ice. They key is to keep the turkey and brine cold at refrigerator temperature.

After 24 hours in the brine, remove the turkey and discard the brine. Rinse the turkey and pat dry. Lay out the turkey on a baking sheet and put it in the refrigerator, uncovered, for 1 hour to dry the turkey.

Remove the turkey from the refrigerator and pat dry one more time. A dry turkey is important when seasoning. To season the turkey, flip it breast side down. Coat the bottom of the turkey with half of the oil and half of the Poultry Rub. Flip the turkey over and repeat on the breast side.

Prepare the smoker to 275 degrees F using hickorywood. Place the turkey on the smoker, breast side up and laid out with the drumsticks facing toward each other and the wing tips tucked under the breastbone (see the photo on page 102). Insert two meat thermometer probes, if possible, one into the breast and the other into the drumstick to monitor the temperature.

Remove the turkey from the smoker when the internal temperature of the breast and thighs is 165 degrees F. Let sit for 20 minutes, then carve and serve.

WINE PAIRING: The holiday bird is one of many flavorful foods on the table competing for attention. When it comes to pairing wine with a holiday meal, such as Thanksgiving, our rule of thumb is to have at least one crowd-friendly white wine (such as chardonnay or riesling), one all-purpose red (like pinot noir or zinfandel), and always a sparkling wine (domestic sparkling wines are our preference for this holiday, either from Oregon or California). All of these will work wonders with the turkey, as well as with the typical side dishes.

KING OF MEATS: BEEF

Our guidelines for cooking beef are simple: start with the best quality you can get your hands on, followed by simple seasoning. For whole steak cuts, we like to reverse sear to add a smoke element to the meat before searing. When marinating, we make sure to avoid too much time in the marinade so we can still taste the meaty flavor. When adding beef to a dish, like a lasagne, we add a simple smoke element to enhance the flavor versus overpowering the entire dish.

Portion size is also something to consider. One large steak may look exciting on a plate, but we typically allocate a one-half pound of beef per person. So, when considering purchasing your cuts, one steak may actually feed two people.

When it comes to finished cooking temperature, we like our steaks rare to medium rare. We mention this so you can modify your desired finished temperature to however you prefer your beef, whether it's medium to well done.

Experiment with your local butcher, and don't be afraid to ask for cuts you aren't familiar with.

DONENESS	TEMPERATURE (IN DEGREES F)	
Rare	120 to 130	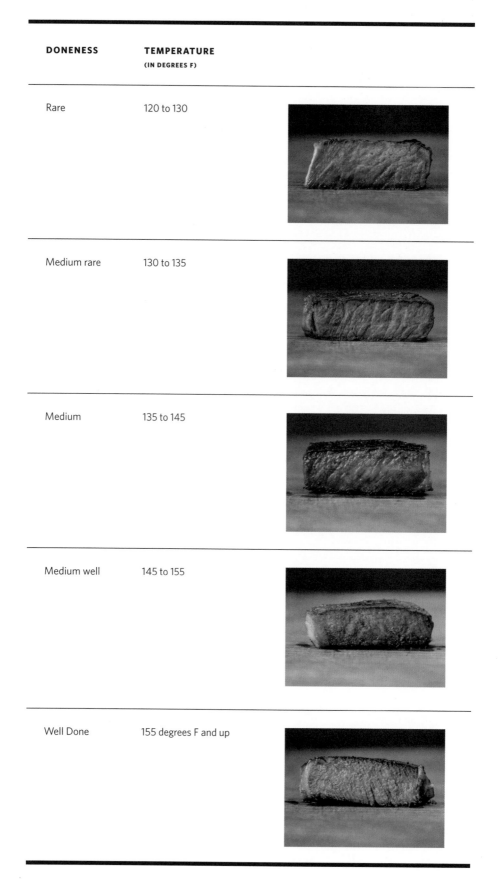
Medium rare	130 to 135	
Medium	135 to 145	
Medium well	145 to 155	
Well Done	155 degrees F and up	

REVERSE SEARED RIB EYES

You might be noticing a theme around big steak cuts: adding a smoke flavor first, then finishing over high heat, which offers the best of both styles of cooking. Top with a compound butter and you have an amazing balance of butter, salt, savory, smoke, and beefy flavor. We serve the steaks sliced, so often we buy two large, thick steaks for four people.

MAKES 4 SERVINGS

For the compound butter
- 1 stick (4 ounces) unsalted butter, at room temperature
- 1½ teaspoons minced garlic
- 1 teaspoon finely chopped fresh rosemary
- ¼ teaspoon kosher salt
- Cooking spray

For the steaks
- 2 (1-pound) bone-in rib-eye steaks, at least 1½ inches thick
- 2 tablespoons extra-virgin olive oil
- 2 tablespoons Beef Rub (page 63)

To make the compound butter, in a small bowl, add the butter, garlic, rosemary, and salt. Using your hands or a strong spatula, combine the ingredients. Lay out a piece of plastic wrap and coat with cooking spray. Place the butter on the plastic wrap and form into your desired shape. We roll it into a log, wrap tightly, and keep it in the refrigerator for up to 5 days.

To prepare the steaks, coat the rib eyes with the oil and Beef Rub. Cover and place them in the refrigerator for up to 2 hours.

Preheat the smoker to 225 degrees F using oak or hickory, and remove the steaks from the refrigerator.

Smoke the steaks for 45 minutes to 1 hour, or until the internal temperature is 112 degrees F.

As the steaks near the final smoke temperature, prepare the grill for direct cooking or heat a large cast-iron skillet over high heat.

After removing the steaks from the smoker, place them on direct heat on the grill or in the skillet to sear for 3 minutes. Flip and sear another 3 minutes. We pull our steaks when the internal temperature is 125 degrees F in the center of the steak.

Remove the steaks and add 1 tablespoon of the compound butter over the top of each. The butter will start to melt immediately. Allow the steaks to rest for 10 minutes before cutting.

WINE PAIRING: The sweet kiss of smoke, the hearty, mouthwatering meat, and the flavorful butter sauce are a match made in heaven for a cabernet sauvignon or syrah.

MERLOT SPRITZED BEEF BRISKET

Brisket is one of those BBQ cuts that can intimidate a lot of people. It's expensive, and no two ever cook the same. But when you get it right, the flavor and the texture make every hour you spent preparing worth it. With brisket, the technique in how you prepare and the milestones you keep an eye out for while it goes through its cook are the most important parts of understanding how to perfect your brisket.

MAKES 16 TO 20 SERVINGS

1 (12- to 14-pound) packer (whole) brisket

¼ cup extra-virgin olive oil

1 cup Beef Rub (page 63)

Merlot Wine Spritz (page 68)

The night before cooking, trim the excess fat off the brisket (see page 117). Coat brisket with the oil and liberally apply the Beef Rub. Depending on the size of your brisket, you may or may not use all the rub. Be sure to apply the rub on the sides and into any pockets. Wrap the brisket in aluminum foil or plastic wrap and place it in the refrigerator overnight.

Remove the brisket from refrigerator and unwrap. Preheat your smoker to 250 degrees F. We use fruitwood, such as apple or cherry.

Place the brisket on the smoker and insert your two-zone meat probes. One is for the meat inserted into the flat, and one is to monitor the ambient temperature of the cooking chamber and is not inserted into the meat.

After 2 hours, begin spritzing the brisket with the Merlot Wine Spritz. Spritz every 30 minutes until you wrap. The liquid you are spraying helps the smoke to adhere to the meat and create more flavor.

When the internal temperature of the brisket is 165 degrees F, the brisket is going into a process called *the stall*. This is the period in which the meat sweats internally; the moisture from the intramuscular fat is rendering and the meat is reacting to the temperature inside the cooking chamber, like sweat. So the rise in internal temperature slows down. This is the point where we wrap the brisket. See page 116 for photo instructions.

Carefully remove the brisket, to avoid disturbing the crust, or *bark*, that has formed, and place onto two pieces of pink butcher paper to wrap. You can also use aluminum foil. Remove the meat probe, tightly wrap the brisket, and then add the meat probe back into the same general area. Place the brisket back into the smoker. This can take 4 to 7 hours to reach 165 degrees F from the start of the cook.

Continue cooking at 250 degrees F wrapped for several more hours until the brisket approaches 195 degrees F. You know the stall is over when the internal temperature starts to rise quickly. At that point, use your instant-read thermometer to insert and probe the flat and the point for a smooth, buttery texture. The thermometer should ease

→

in with no tension. The brisket may be done at anywhere from 195 to 205 degrees F. This is the time to be patient, as you will get temperatures across the range in various areas. The key is getting the proper texture and temperature at the center of the point and the flat consistently.

Remove the brisket from the smoker when the thermometer inserts smoothly, like a knife through butter. Leaving it wrapped, let it rest for 1 hour in a cooler (with no ice) to hold the temperature until ready to serve. The meat will stay warm for up to 4 hours with the right size cooler.

Slice against the grain and serve.

NOTE: One side of the brisket has a fat layer. Depending on your cooker, the fat side should face the hotter portion of your smoker. So, in the case of our Big Green Egg, we cook fat side down because it is hotter from the bottom of the smoker. For our offset smoker, we cook fat-side up. This fat layer will protect the meat from the heat for a more even cook.

WINE PAIRING: This is one of the holy grails of BBQ and time to let the meat get all the glory and be the star of the show. The meat is rich, smoky, and should be mouthwatering. Tempranillo goes with brisket, as well as Washington State syrah and Rhône-style blends. We're not going to lie though; after a day of smoking this beast, we've been known to pop open a refreshing and fruity rosé to reward our efforts. It also livens up your palate from each bite of the buttery rich meat.

Wrapping Brisket

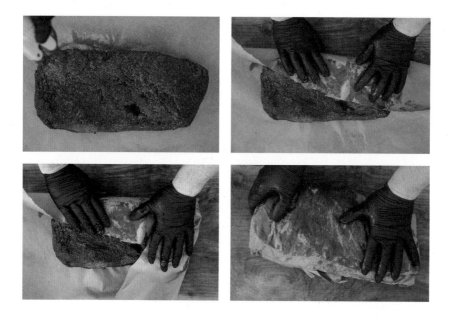

Trimming Instructions

One of the first and important steps in brisket, besides meat quality, is trimming. A whole packer brisket is made up of two muscles from the breast of the cow. There is the point, a well-marbled angled part of the brisket that is often cut up for burnt ends, and the flat, the leaner cut of the brisket that runs underneath the point and creates the length. A thin layer of fat separates the point from the flat. We follow a few key steps to trim without taking forever to do it.

Start with the brisket flat side up. There will be some membrane and silverskin and a few pockets of fat you want to make sure are removed. Next, look at the two sides of the brisket. You'll see some overlapping fat from the point on either side. We typically cut off about ¼ inch of meat on either side, which exposes the meat and marbling.

Flip the brisket and start to trim up the point. This is the area with the most amount of fat. First, you'll see some bumpy, thick, and hard fat. That won't render when cooking, so remove all of that. Typically, it's on top of the point and on the front edges. Next, remove the fat from along the top of the brisket, leaving about ¼ inch of the fat layer.

Finally, there are pockets along the edges and into the point that require getting into and continuing to chip away at that thick dense fat that won't render. Remember that a line of this fat separates the point from the flat, so you won't remove all of it, but you can square up the edges and corners by slowly cutting into the meat and taking the hard fat out until you start seeing pockets of the beef.

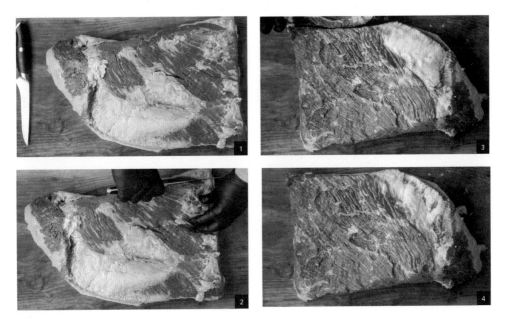

1 Make sure the fat cap is facing up.
2 Trim fat off both edges, then remove the fat cap, leaving a fat layer of no more than a ¼ inch.
3 Flip the brisket to the flat side and remove excess silverskin.
4 Remove any excess fat, as shown in the upper right.

THE TOMAHAWK

The dramatic look of a tomahawk is nothing short of jaw-dropping. This is something you have to try at least once. If anything, just think of the Instagram photos you'll get out of it. The tomahawk is simply a long-bone version of the rib steak, or rib eye, trimmed and made for dramatic presentation. Because of the bone, you will find that tomahawks are at least two inches thick, are the perfect cut for a reverse sear, and are definitely fun to serve with company. The only problem is determining who gets to keep the bone.

MAKES 4 SERVINGS

1 (3- to 4-pound) tomahawk steak (note that the bone will be at least 1 pound when determining portions)

1½ tablespoons extra-virgin olive oil

2 tablespoons Beef Rub (see page 71)

Brush the tomahawk with the oil and liberally apply the Beef Rub. It is recommended to do this 1 day in advance and refrigerate.

Preheat the smoker to 250 degrees F using hickorywood or oakwood.

Smoke for 1 hour to 90 minutes, or until the internal temperature is 118 to 120 degrees F measured in the center of the cut.

Set your grill for direct heat as your steak approaches 118 to 120 degrees F. Remove the steak from the smoker, then add it to the direct heat for the final sear. Cook for 4 to 5 minutes, flip, and cook another 4 to 5 minutes, or until the internal temperature is 125 degrees F for rare.

If you like your steak cooked to medium, smoke until the internal temperature is 125 degrees F, then sear until your desired doneness based on internal temperature. Remove the steak from the grill. Let it rest 10 minutes before slicing.

WINE PAIRING: The tomahawk is definitely going to steal the show here. But you're more than welcome to partner it with your prizeworthy cabernet sauvignon or Bordeaux-style blend. The meat is rich with plenty of fat to smooth out any tannins from the wine.

SKIRT STEAK GRILLED FLATBREAD

Flatbread, to us, is a fancy way of saying pizza without the red sauce. It also is a lot of fun in the summer when we can all hang out outside and get friends and family to help make their own versions of this great treat. We don't go overboard when it comes to toppings for our flatbreads, for ease of transferring them on and off the grill. The flavor of the beef after marinating is tasty enough to dress this flatbread. The rest of the toppings just enhance the experience.

MAKES ONE 10- TO 12-INCH FLATBREAD

For the marinade
- ½ cup extra-virgin olive oil
- ¼ cup lager beer
- 3 tablespoons Worcestershire sauce
- 2 tablespoons chopped shallots
- 1 tablespoon Dijon mustard
- 1 clove garlic, crushed
- 1 teaspoon balsamic vinegar
- ½ teaspoon kosher salt
- ½ teaspoon coarse black pepper
- ½ teaspoon red chili pepper flakes

For the steak
- 1 pound skirt steak

- 1 tablespoon Beef Rub (page 71)

For the flatbread
- 1 store-bought pizza dough
- 1 tablespoon cornmeal or all-purpose flour, for the peel
- 1 cup cherry tomatoes, halved
- ¼ cup blue cheese
- ¼ cup Parmesan cheese
- ¼ cup Smoked Pickled Onions (recipe follows)
- 2 cups arugula
- Aged balsamic vinegar, for drizzling
- 1 teaspoon finishing salt

To make the marinade, mix all of the ingredients in a 1-gallon ziplock bag.

To prepare the steak, trim the steak of any excess fat, then place it in the bag with the marinade for up to 2 hours.

Prepare the grill for direct/indirect cooking.

Remove the steak from the marinade and pat dry. Season with the Beef Rub.

Grill the steak over direct heat and cover, 4 to 6 minutes. Flip and grill, covered, for 4 to 6 minutes, or until the internal temperature is at least 125 degrees F. This is a thin cut, so it will grill fast and will continue to cook on the flatbread.

Remove the steak from the grill, let rest for 5 minutes, then cut it into thin slices.

Meanwhile, modify the grill with a pizza stone or steel, according to the manufacturer's suggestion. Add more charcoal if needed.

$\longrightarrow$

When grilling pizza on a stone, it is best to have the stone over an indirect heat source or some type of plate that will deflect the direct heat from the stone. Do not place the stone directly over a flame. If using a kettle grill with no diffuser, we push the coals along two sides of the grill to accomplish the same task. The target temperature is 500 degrees F.

To prepare the flatbread, roll out the pizza dough on a smooth surface to 10 to 12 inches.

Dust a pizza peel with the cornmeal; this will help the flatbread to slide off the peel. Lay out the rolled dough on the peel, then top with the steak, tomatoes, blue cheese, Parmesan, and Smoked Pickled Onions.

Transfer the flatbread onto the pizza stone and cover. At 500 degrees F, the flatbread will cook in 6 to 8 minutes. Pull the flatbread when you see a nice crust form. Top with the arugula, drizzle with vinegar, and dust with the finishing salt.

WINE PAIRING: There are a lot of fun flavors going on here, from the savory meat to the pickled onions to the pungent cheese. If you want to keep it simple, opt for a fruity, bold-style rosé. For reds, malbec and fruity gamay work well.

Smoked Pickled Onions

These smoked pickled onions have become such a staple at our house that we always have a jar of them in our fridge. Use them to enhance everyday staples like tacos, burgers, wraps, salads, and more. We use them on so many things that we had to include them in this book. You'll thank us later when you find yourself adding a few of these to your weeknight meals.

MAKES 2 CUPS

½ cup apple cider vinegar

2 tablespoons cane sugar

1 tablespoon kosher salt

2 cups thinly sliced red onions

Preheat the smoker to 225 degrees F using applewood.

In a 2-quart smoker-safe dish, add the vinegar, sugar, and salt. Stir to mix and dissolve.

Add the onions to the pickling liquid and place on the smoker for 3 hours. Remove and strain the liquid. If not using right away, store in an airtight container in the refrigerator for up to 4 weeks.

SMOKED BEEF LASAGNE

Nothing says comfort food like a huge and hearty dish of lasagne. We love a lasagne jam-packed with meaty flavors and lots of sauce. This one combines ground beef, spicy Italian pork, and mushrooms for a meaty and smoky experience. When smoked, the three create an incredible trinity of flavors to use as a base for this symphony of a dish. Make sure you use a big enough casserole dish because there is nothing skimping on this lasagne. It's meaty, saucy, cheesy, and ultradelicious.

MAKES 6 TO 8 SERVINGS

For the meat and portobello

1 pound ground beef, 80 percent lean/
    20 percent fat
1 pound hot Italian ground pork
1 tablespoon plus 1 teaspoon Beef Rub
    (page 63)
1 large portobello mushroom
1½ teaspoons extra-virgin olive oil

For the sauce

1 tablespoon extra-virgin olive oil
1 small yellow onion, chopped
2 cloves garlic, chopped
1 cup dry red wine
1 (28-ounce) can San Marzano tomatoes (if
    using whole, pulse in a blender)

2 (15-ounce) cans tomato sauce
1 tablespoon fresh chopped basil
½ teaspoon kosher salt
¼ teaspoon red chili pepper flakes
¼ teaspoon coarse ground black pepper

For the filling and assembly

1 (15-ounce) container ricotta cheese
1½ cups Parmesan cheese, divided
1 egg
1 (10-ounce) package no-boil lasagne
    noodles (12 sheets)
4 cups shredded mozzarella cheese,
    divided

Preheat the smoker to 250 degrees F.

To prepare the meat and portobello, distribute the uncooked ground beef and pork on a baking sheet that will fit in your smoker. Season the beef and pork with 1 tablespoon of the Beef Rub.

Remove the stem of the portobello. Using a spoon, scrape off the gills from the cap and discard. Season the portobello with the oil and the remaining 1 teaspoon of the Beef Rub.

Place the baking sheet with the beef, pork, and portobello on the smoker and cook until the temperature of the meat is 160 degrees F, 45 minutes to 1 hour, and until the portobello is fork-tender, 30 to 40 minutes.

Remove the baking sheet from the smoker, then cut up the portobello into small chunks and set aside.

$\longrightarrow$

To make the sauce, in a medium Dutch oven (or equivalent) over medium heat, add the oil and then the onions. Stir until softened, 4 to 5 minutes, then add the garlic and stir 1 minute, or until soft. Add the meat and portobello. Cook 3 minutes to get some browning into the pot, then add the wine. Turn up the heat to bring the wine to a simmer. After 2 minutes of simmering, add the tomatoes, tomato sauce, basil, salt, pepper flakes, and black pepper.

Let the sauce simmer for 20 to 30 minutes. Remove from the heat.

To make the filling, in a large bowl, combine the ricotta, 1 cup of the Parmesan, and the egg. Stir until smooth.

Preheat the oven (or grill) to 375 degrees F.

To assemble the lasagne, use a 9-by-13-inch baking dish. Start by spreading 1½ cups of the sauce in the dish as the base. Arrange 3 noodles on top of the sauce. Add ⅔ cup of the filling and gently spread over the noodles. Sprinkle with 1 cup of the mozzarella. Repeat the layering of sauce, noodles, filling, and mozzarella two more times. Top with the remaining noodles, sauce, 1 cup of the mozzarella, and ½ cup of the Parmesan.

Cover with aluminum foil and bake for 40 minutes. Remove the foil and turn up the temperature to 400 degrees F. Bake for 15 to 20 minutes, or until the cheese is golden. Remove from the oven and let sit for 20 minutes before slicing and serving.

WINE PAIRING: Go Italian with this dish. There's just something about a hearty, saucy, cheesy pasta dish and a fruity barbera or high-acid Chianti to bring it all together. Branching outside of Italy, look for zinfandel or sangiovese from eastern Oregon.

SMOKED MEATLOAF

When we were growing up, meatloaf was an easy weekday dinner. By adding smoked flavor with high-quality ground beef and a cherry glaze at the end, you suddenly take this traditional comfort food to a whole other level.

MAKES 6 SERVINGS

For the glaze
- ½ cup ketchup
- ¼ cup fruity red wine such as malbec, merlot, or zinfandel
- 2 tablespoons cherry jam

For the meatloaf
- 1 cup diced onions
- 1 tablespoon extra-virgin olive oil
- 2 cloves garlic, minced

- ¼ cup chicken stock
- 1 tablespoon tomato paste
- 1 tablespoon Worcestershire sauce
- 1 pound ground beef, 80 percent lean/ 20 percent fat
- 1 pound hot Italian bulk pork sausage
- 1 egg
- ¾ cup panko bread crumbs
- ⅓ cup shredded Parmesan cheese

To make the glaze, in a small saucepan over medium heat, combine the ketchup, wine, and jam until it starts to simmer. Reduce the heat and cook for 4 minutes (avoid boiling).

Let the glaze cool in the refrigerator for at least 30 minutes. If it's hot when you apply it to the meatloaf, it will run right off.

Preheat the smoker to 250 degrees F using fruitwood (we like cherry).

To make the meatloaf, in a large sauté pan over medium heat, add the onions and oil and cook for 5 minutes, or until the onions are soft but not caramelized. Add the garlic and cook 1 minute. Turn off the heat, and mix in the chicken stock, tomato paste, and Worcestershire sauce. Stir and set aside.

In a large bowl, combine the beef, sausage, onion mixture, egg, bread crumbs, and Parmesan. Mix with your hands to incorporate.

Place parchment paper on a baking sheet that will fit into your smoker. On the parchment, form the loaf into a rectangle; it should be roughly 9 inches long and 2 inches tall.

Smoke for 60 minutes, or until the internal temperature is 150 degrees F measured in the center of the loaf. Apply half of the glaze to the meatloaf, then continue smoking 30 minutes, or until the internal temperature of the meatloaf is 165 degrees F. Remove and apply the remainder of the glaze while the meatloaf cools, about 10 minutes.

Slice and serve.

WINE PAIRING: Too sweet of a ketchup topping can kill some wine options. But not when wine is *in* the sauce to balance out the flavor! Sangiovese, Spanish garnacha (or grenache), Côtes du Rhône, a young Rioja, or a Washington State merlot will all work well with the juicy meat and flavorful topping.

WINE-BRAISED SMOKED BEEF SHORT RIBS

Mary spent the better part of her twenties as a pseudo-vegetarian (OK, so she cheated occasionally!). It wasn't until her meat epiphany at a restaurant in Honolulu, called Chef Mavro, that she switched back. It was a single cut of meat that worked its magic—a braised short ribs dish that was so tender it melted in her mouth like butter. She had never tasted anything like it in her life. It was life changing, and she promised that day if she could learn to cook meat this good that she'd convert back to the dark side. She hasn't looked back. To this day, short ribs are Mary's all-time favorite cut of beef, and this method is her kryptonite.

MAKES 4 TO 6 SERVINGS

For the short ribs
- 3 to 4 pounds beef short ribs
- ¼ cup extra-virgin olive oil
- ½ cup Beef Rub (page 63)

For the spritz
- ⅓ cup beef broth
- ⅓ cup dry red wine
- ⅓ cup Worcestershire sauce

For the braising liquid
- 1 cup dry red wine
- 1 cup beef broth
- 1 tablespoon Beef Rub (page 63)
- 2 tablespoons unsalted butter

Preheat the smoker to 225 degrees F using fruitwood.

To prepare the short ribs, trim off the silverskin. Coat the short ribs with the oil and season liberally with the Beef Rub. (Depending on the size of your short ribs, you may or may not use all of the Beef Rub; just make sure it's applied liberally.)

Place the short ribs on the smoker.

To prepare the spritz, in a medium bowl, mix the broth, wine, and Worcestershire sauce. Transfer it to a food-safe spray bottle.

After the short ribs have been cooking for 2 hours, begin spritzing them until just damp every 30 minutes for 1 to 2 additional hours. Look for the meat pulling back from the bone and a good mahogany color as indicators it is ready for the braise. When the internal temperature is roughly 165 degrees F (3 to 4 hours on smoke), transfer the short ribs to an aluminum pan.

$\longrightarrow$

To the pan, add the braising ingredients: the wine, broth, Beef Rub, and butter. Gently mix together. Cover tightly with aluminum foil and place back into the smoker.

After 1 hour, use a meat thermometer to probe the short ribs. The short ribs are done when the thermometer inserts smoothly, like a knife through butter. There should not be much resistance; if it's not like butter, it is not quite done so keep cooking until it is.

Once you have determined the short ribs are done (roughly 200 to 205 degrees F), remove from the smoker and let sit, covered, for 15 minutes.

Remove the short ribs from the braising liquid. Serve with a root vegetable puree, mashed potatoes, or creamy polenta to soak up all the intoxicating juices that will flow from the tender meat.

WINE PAIRING: For this dish, choose something full bodied but not overly intense. We like some acid to refresh the palate. A Sonoma Valley cabernet sauvignon is perfect for this, tempranillo from Ribera del Duero, as well as a Washington State syrah.

SKIRT STEAK STREET TACOS

Street tacos are all about simple flavors that reflect authenticity. They feature marinated meats in a warm corn tortilla, lightly complemented with onion and a few extra ingredients. Keep it simple with this full-flavored preparation for your next Taco Tuesday.

MAKES 4 TO 6 SERVINGS

For the steak
 1 pound skirt steak
 ½ cup freshly squeezed navel orange juice
  (2 large oranges)
 ¼ cup freshly squeezed lime juice (from 2
  medium limes)
 ¼ cup roughly chopped white onion
 2 tablespoons chopped jalapeño pepper
 1 tablespoon minced garlic
 ½ teaspoon ground black pepper
 ½ teaspoon kosher salt
 ½ teaspoon chili powder

 ¼ teaspoon cumin
 1 tablespoon Beef Rub (page 63)

For the pico de gallo
 ¾ cup diced fresh tomatoes
 ½ cup diced white onion
 2 tablespoons chopped fresh cilantro
 1 tablespoon chopped jalapeño pepper
 1½ teaspoons minced garlic
 1½ teaspoons freshly squeezed lime juice
 ¼ teaspoon kosher salt, plus more to taste
 8 to 12 corn tortillas

To prepare the skirt steak, trim off any excess fat or silverskin from both sides of the steak. If the steak is one long piece, consider cutting it into 8-inch lengths for marinating and grilling ease.

In a 1-gallon ziplock bag, mix the orange juice, lime juice, onion, jalapeño, garlic, black pepper, salt, chili powder, and cumin. Place the steak in the bag, let out as much air as possible, and lock the bag. Let the steak marinate in the refrigerator for at least 1 hour but no more than 6 hours.

Prepare the grill for direct cooking.

Remove the steak from bag and pat dry. Discard the marinade. Season the steak with the Beef Rub on both sides.

Place the steak on the grill and close the lid. Cook for 5 minutes, or until you have a nice sear. Flip the steak and cook for 4 to 5 minutes, or until an instant-read thermometer reads 125 to 130 degrees F.

Remove the steak from the grill and let sit for 10 minutes. While the steak is resting, prepare the pico de gallo.

$\longrightarrow$

To make the pico de gallo, combine the tomatoes, onions, cilantro, jalapeño, garlic, lime juice, and salt in a medium bowl. Stir and add more salt to taste.

For a good bite of steak in the taco, slice it thinly. The best method is to cut the steak into 4-inch squares. Then turn the steak so you can cut perpendicular to the muscle striations. Slice as thinly as possible at a 45-degree angle.

To prepare the tacos, fill each corn tortilla with steak and pico de gallo. Add any other favorite toppings. We love to add a squeeze of lime and some freshly chopped cilantro.

WINE PAIRING: On nine Taco Tuesdays out of ten, we're sipping a fruity rosé. Other times we reach for a light-bodied, fresh, acidic red wine to balance out the flavors from the savory marinade and freshness of the pico de gallo. Gamay (or Beaujolais), a youthful Rioja (tempranillo), Spanish garnacha, and even carménère work well.

SANTA MARIA–STYLE GRILLED TRI TIP

One of our all-time favorite cuts of beef, tri tip made its claim to fame in California, where this unique cut was singled out as a great alternative to more expensive primal (or most important or first) cuts. Santa Maria is the town where it was alleged to have been made famous. Today you will see a host of styles and seasonings that tie back to Santa Maria–style tri tip. Ours is really focusing on the meat, with some savory and herbal characteristics to balance out the heat. There's a good reason this is the number one cut of beef we serve at events. Find out why.

MAKES 6 SERVINGS

1½ teaspoons kosher salt

1 teaspoon smoked paprika

1 teaspoon coarse ground black pepper

½ teaspoon granulated garlic

½ teaspoon red chili pepper flakes

½ teaspoon dried oregano

½ teaspoon dried thyme

1 tri tip (averages about 1½ pounds)

1 tablespoon extra-virgin olive oil

Prepare the grill for direct/indirect cooking.

In a small bowl, mix the salt, paprika, black pepper, garlic, pepper flakes, oregano, and thyme.

Coat the tri tip with the oil and liberally apply the dry rub to all sides.

Place the tri tip over direct heat for 4 to 6 minutes, then flip for another 4 to 6 minutes. Once you have a nice seared look on both sides, move the tri tip to the indirect side. Cover and cook until the internal temperature is 127 degrees F, about 10 minutes. Remove from the grill and let sit for 10 minutes.

When slicing tri tip, you will see that it has three directional striations to the muscle. You want to be sure to slice perpendicular to the muscle striations, cutting against the grain.

WINE PAIRING: This style of tri tip has its roots in the Santa Barbara wine region. To honor that, we're going with a syrah from Santa Barbara County. Malbec or tempranillo would be a close second.

SMOKEHOUSE BURGERS

Go to any smokehouse or tavern and you may see a smoky burger. Our take is to actually smoke the patty (versus grilling it) and layer flavor through the toppings. Bacon is key, as is our Smoked Pickled Onions (page 122). Finally, we use brioche for our bun. Buttery and fluffy, it just soaks up the juices. We really like a simple burger, as the beef flavor is most important. With the added smoke element, this burger typifies authentic backyard cooking with a family feel.

MAKES 4 BURGERS

8 slices thick-cut bacon

1¼ pounds ground beef, 80 percent lean/20 percent fat

1 tablespoon Beef Rub (page 63)

1 egg, beaten

1½ teaspoons Worcestershire sauce

4 slices sharp cheddar cheese

4 brioche buns

1 bunch butter lettuce

½ cup Pinot Noir BBQ Sauce (page 66) or your favorite Kansas City–style sauce

¼ cup Smoked Pickled Onions (page 122)

Preheat the smoker to 250 degrees F using applewood or oakwood. Put the bacon in the smoker as it will take up to 90 minutes to get crispy skin.

In a large bowl, combine the beef, Beef Rub, egg, and Worcestershire sauce. Mix with your hands and make 4 equal-size patties. Each will be a little over ¼ pound. Chef's trick: using an oiled ramekin is a great way to form an even patty.

Place the burgers on the smoker and smoke for 1 hour, or until the internal temperature of the beef is 155 degrees F. Place a slice of cheese on each. We do this while the bacon is smoking.

Continue cooking another 10 minutes, or until the internal temperature is 160 degrees F. Remove from the smoker and construct the burgers.

On top of the base bun, place a leaf of the lettuce, then the burger. Add 1 tablespoon (or more if desired) of the Pinot Noir BBQ Sauce, then a few Smoked Pickled Onions and the bun top.

WINE PAIRING: The bold, rich, and smoky flavors here call for a bold wine. California zinfandel, GSM (grenache, syrah, mourvedre) blends from Washington State, petite sirah, tempranillo from Ribera del Duero, and even monastrell (mourvedre from Spain) are good choices.

NEW YORK STRIP WITH SAVORY DUCK FAT GRANOLA

Instead of using a sauce or relish for a steak topping, consider something that adds flavor, plus a little texture and extra wow factor. Here we are adding a savory component to a granola to use as a topping. We've served this at a number of public events and love the feedback when customers don't know what to expect. The granola is slightly crunchy and sweet, with a finish of thyme and a savory mouthfeel from the duck fat.

MAKES 4 SERVINGS WITH GRANOLA LEFTOVER

For the granola
- ¼ cup duck fat (see note, page 136)
- ¼ cup finely chopped shallots
- 2¼ cups rolled oats
- ¼ cup cane sugar
- 1½ teaspoons chopped fresh thyme
- 1 teaspoon kosher salt

For the steaks
- 2 (1-pound) New York strip steaks, 1½ inches thick
- 2 tablespoons extra-virgin olive oil
- 2 tablespoons Beef Rub (page 63)
- Olive oil, for the pan

To make the granola, preheat the oven to 200 degrees F. In a large skillet over medium heat, heat the duck fat until melted. Add the shallots and stir. Cook for 3 minutes, or until the shallots are softened.

Reduce the heat to low and add the oats, sugar, thyme, and salt. Whisk until the oats are lightly toasted and the duck fat and caramelized sugar have been incorporated.

Remove from the heat. On a baking sheet lined with parchment paper, spread out the granola evenly. Bake for 1 hour, then stir to redistribute the granola. Bake for another 40 minutes.

Remove from the oven. The granola will look slightly toasted and the oats will be firm but not browned. You can make the granola in advance. Store in an airtight container for up to 2 months.

To make the steaks, preheat the smoker to 225 degrees F using oak or hickory.

$\longrightarrow$

Coat the steaks with the oil and Beef Rub. Place them on the smoker for up to 1 hour, or until the internal temperature of the steaks is 112 degrees F.

Remove the steaks from the smoker. Prepare the grill for direct cooking or heat a large cast-iron skillet over high heat. Place the steaks on direct heat for 4 minutes, then flip. Cook for 3 minutes, or until the internal temperature of the steaks is 124 degrees F. If using a skillet, add a little oil first and cook the steak for a total of 7 minutes, as above.

Remove the steaks from the heat and let rest for 10 minutes. Slice the steaks. Cover each portion with 1 tablespoon of the granola and serve.

NOTE: Duck fat can be purchased at a specialty store. You can also make your own home-made duck fat by slowly rendering pieces of duck skin over the course of several hours.

WINE PAIRING: We're looking for a red wine with enough structure and power to stand up to the bold flavors of this steak without overpowering the delicate flavors of the savory granola. Southern Rhône reds work great, as do tempranillo from Ribera del Duero.

PORKLANDIA

We are very fortunate in the Pacific Northwest to have access to some amazing pork farmers. Early on in our cooking days, pork was our favorite protein to cook. Ribs and pork shoulder are staples at any of our personal and professional events. Our pork dishes are a nod to those from the Carolinas, where the sauces are similar to our preferences. A lot of whole hog and pork cooking happens there, which naturally had an influence on us.

One of our favorite public events to cook at is the annual Porklandia event, a celebration in Carlton, Oregon, of all things pig. The town gets together over Father's Day weekend and features pork dishes and local food, wine, and crafts. We have fun creating unique dishes that reflect how versatile pork and various pork cuts can be presented. This is where we introduced our Pork Belly Burnt Ends (page 153) in 2016.

Whether jazzing up an old-school pork chop recipe or finding new flavors to add to ribs, pork is a blast to work with!

3-2-1 RIBS

We get a lot of questions about the easiest way to cook ribs. This is one of the most common methods we recommend as you start out and get to know your cooker and preferred style of ribs. The numbers represent the initial smoke time (three hours), followed by time spent wrapped in foil (two hours), and smoke time again, unwrapped, with a sauce (one hour). Sometimes people will opt for a four-one-one or two-two-two combination. It really comes down to your preference of smoke flavor and texture. The key, though, is knowing the cooking order: smoke to wrap to smoke again with a sauce to finish.

We use St. Louis–style ribs, where some of the extra flap meat is already trimmed off of a full spare, making it easier for you.

MAKES 6 TO 8 SERVINGS

For the ribs
2 racks St. Louis-style spareribs
4 tablespoons Dijon mustard
4 tablespoons Sweet Rub (page 62)

For the spritz
1 cup apple cider vinegar
1 cup apple juice

For the wrap (at the 3-hour mark)
4 tablespoons unsalted butter, cut into 8 equal pieces
4 tablespoons honey or agave nectar

For the glaze
1 cup Pinot Noir BBQ Sauce (page 66) or your favorite BBQ sauce

Preheat the smoker to 250 degrees F (we like cherrywood or applewood).

To prepare the ribs, trim the excess fat and remove the silverskin from the bone side of the ribs using a paper towel.

Pat the ribs dry using a paper towel, then coat both sides of the ribs with the Dijon, 1 tablespoon per side. Apply the Sweet Rub to both sides, 1 tablespoon per side. Do this at least 1 hour before cooking or the night before.

Place the ribs meat side up on the smoker. Plan to smoke for about 3 hours.

To make the spritz, combine the vinegar and apple juice in a food-safe spray bottle. After the first 90 minutes, start spritzing the ribs every 20 to 30 minutes. Minimize how long you keep the lid open.

After the third hour, lay out two long strips of aluminum foil. Place the ribs on them bone side down.

$\longrightarrow$

To make the wrap, distribute 2 tablespoons of the butter (4 pieces) evenly over the top of each rack of ribs. Drizzle 2 tablespoons of the honey evenly over the meat side of each rack. Squirt a few times with the spritz, then wrap the ribs tightly. Place them back on the smoker meat side down for 2 more hours to allow the butter and honey to steam the ribs.

After the second hour wrapped, gently remove the ribs from the foil. The meat should be tender and the bones pulling back.

For the glaze, use a silicone brush to apply BBQ sauce to the bone side, then flip and apply sauce to the meat side (you may not need the entire 1 cup BBQ sauce). Place back on the smoker, meat side up, and cook for 1 hour, uncovered. The last hour helps set the meat and give it more flavor. Remove from the heat and lightly glaze with more BBQ sauce one more time. Serve immediately.

WINE PAIRING: Pork (ribs in particular) is almost always an appropriate pairing for a fruity pinot noir. This is especially true if you use the recommended Pinot Noir BBQ Sauce. Pork and pinot are a great match, and ribs are no exception with this mild sauce. If you use a bolder Kansas City–style sauce, opt for a zinfandel or malbec. If you use a more acidic sauce, such as the Honey Gold Sauce (page 63), for example, try a domestic sparkling wine (bubbly rosé works great).

How to Trim St. Louis–Style Ribs

St. Louis–style ribs are spareribs that have been precut for you. Even precut, there is still some additional cleanup you can do to maximize tenderness. On the bone side of the ribs, there may be a flap of meat that is hanging over at an angle to the bone. You want to cut this off completely. Discard, or smoke on the side and eat as a snack.

Next, remove the silverskin or membrane from the bone side of the ribs. Using a sharp knife, remove a small corner of the silverskin membrane. Then, using a paper towel, pull the corner away from the bone slowly. Pull it off with one hand, while the other holds the rib down. On the meat side of the ribs, trim any excess fat.

SWEET AND STICKY RIBS

We were inspired to try a hoisin-based glaze for ribs when eating at our local wing shack. They had this amazing sweet and savory spiced wing that exploded with flavor in the mouth. We had to try something like this with ribs. For these, we add Chinese five spice in the dry rub for flavor and a simple sauce of Thai sweet chili sauce, hoisin, and sriracha for kick. Sticky, sweet, and smoky, these define finger licking.

MAKES 6 TO 8 SERVINGS

For the dry rub
- ¼ cup turbinado raw sugar
- 2 tablespoons kosher salt
- 1 tablespoon freshly ground black pepper
- 1½ teaspoons Chinese five spice powder
- 1 teaspoon powdered ginger
- 1 teaspoon granulated garlic
- ¼ teaspoon cayenne pepper

For the ribs
- 2 racks St. Louis–style spareribs
- ¼ cup Dijon mustard
- 4 tablespoons unsalted butter, cut into 8 equal pieces
- 4 tablespoons honey

For the sauce
- ⅔ cup Thai sweet chili sauce
- 2 tablespoons hoisin sauce
- 1 tablespoon sriracha powder

Preheat the smoker to 250 degrees F with fruitwood. We love cherry for this.

To make the dry rub, combine the sugar, salt, black pepper, five spice, ginger, garlic, and cayenne in a small bowl. (This makes a little over ½ cup dry rub; you will not use it all.) Set aside.

To prepare the ribs, trim the excess fat and remove the silverskin from the bone side of the ribs using a paper towel. Pat dry the ribs. Coat both sides with the Dijon, 1 tablespoon per side. Apply the dry rub to both sides, 1 tablespoon per side. Do this at least 1 hour before cooking or the night before.

Place the ribs bone side down on the smoker. We will follow the 3-2-1 method as used for the 3-2-1 Ribs (page 140). Smoke for 3 hours.

The "tell" for moving to the wrap phase is when the meat retracts from the bone about ¼ inch.

After 3 hours, lay out two sheets of aluminum foil overlapping each other. Place one rack of ribs bone side down on the foil. On the meat side of the ribs, apply 2 tablespoons of the butter and 2 tablespoons of the honey. Wrap the ribs, then repeat for the second rack of ribs. Place the ribs back on smoker bone side up for 2 hours. This will allow the butter and honey to baste the ribs. While the ribs are wrapped, make the sauce.

⟶

To make the sauce, combine the chili sauce, hoisin, and sriracha powder in a small bowl.

After 2 hours, remove the ribs from the foil, and apply sauce on both sides. Place the ribs back on the smoker for 30 to 60 minutes, or until the sauce sets or tacks up. Remove from the smoker and add more sauce.

We don't measure the temperature of ribs; instead, we wiggle the rib bones and tend to pull them off the smoker just before those bones are so loose that they pull right out.

Ribs, unlike steaks, can be served immediately, given the amount of cook time and the last portion uncovered. So serve the ribs right away, and make sure you have some Wet-Naps!

WINE PAIRING: With the ribs having a mix of smoke, sweet, savory, and mildly spicy flavors, look for a wine with rich, fruity characteristics that is big enough to stand up to the boldness. However, a wine with strong tannins isn't necessary since most the fat in the ribs will have rendered. A jammy zinfandel works well, but we love a Washington State syrah for this. It is smoky, fruity, powerful, and with enough acidity to round everything out.

SWEET RUB PULLED PORK

One of our favorite things to cook is pork shoulder (also called pork butt and commonly found in a butcher case as Boston butt). No matter what it's called, it is delicious. Like brisket, there is a methodical way to approach the phases of cooking it that includes the smoke, the wrap, and the resting time so you maximize flavor and texture. Pork is great the next day too; something about letting it continue to rest adds to the smoke element and the leftover potential is endless.

We love using a bone-in butt for two reasons. The first is its shape. The shape is relatively uniform, which even after trimming presents an easy way to get smoke rolling over the cut. With boneless, it's not an even shape because the bone has been gouged out, and you don't get as clean of a bark since the butt is cut up. The second reason we like bone-in butt is that we can inject the meat with a liquid mixture using a food-safe syringe much easier. This liquid gets into the center of the meat and adds moisture and flavor where a dry rub couldn't reach. The bone keeps it all together so the added injection doesn't leak out as easily as it would with boneless.

MAKES 10 TO 14 SERVINGS

For the pork
1 (8- to 10-pound) bone-in pork shoulder or Boston butt
¼ cup Dijon mustard
⅔ cup Sweet Rub (page 62)

For the injection
1 cup apple cider vinegar
1 cup apple juice

For the spritz
1 cup apple cider vinegar
1 cup apple juice

Special tool
Meat injector

Prepare the pork the night before cooking. Remove the excess fat cap on top, leaving no more than a ¼-inch fat layer, and any glands. Glands will appear reddish or pink in color and look out of place compared with fat or meat. Rinse with cold water, then place on a baking sheet.

To prepare the injection, combine the vinegar and juice in a large bowl. Draw the vinegar mixture into a meat injector.

Inject the pork. When injecting, think of the pork as a checkerboard. You will insert the probe every few inches and slowly add the liquid throughout the meat. You will see it swell and that is OK. Drain the baking sheet of any excess moisture, and pat the pork dry using a paper towel. Discard any unused injection liquid; do not use it for the spritz, which would become contaminated by liquid that touched raw meat.

⟶

Coat the pork with the Dijon, then apply the Sweet Rub thoroughly. If you don't add them the night before, apply at least 1 hour before cooking. You'll see the rub begin to liquefy as the moisture connects with the meat.

Preheat the smoker to 250 degrees F. We use applewood or cherrywood. Insert a thermometer if you have a remote probe and leave it in place.

Place the pork, fat cap side up, on the smoker and smoke for 3 hours. You'll see a bark begin to develop. While the pork is smoking, make the spritz.

To make the spritz, combine the vinegar and juice in a medium bowl, then transfer to a food-safe squirt bottle. If you don't have a squirt bottle, you can keep it in the bowl and use a food-safe basting brush or basting mop.

After 3 hours, spritz or baste the pork every 30 minutes. Check the temperature of the pork after smoking for about 5 hours. When the pork hits 165 degrees F, it's ready to wrap. This is the point where you can see the stall occur (see The Stall, below).

Wrapping helps push through the stall when you start to see the temperature increase at a much faster pace. To wrap, first remove the meat probe. Next, lay out two large sheets of aluminum foil overlapping each other, and place the pork on the foil. Alternatively, you can use an aluminum pan. Remove the cap of the spray bottle and pour about 2 tablespoons of the spritz over the pork (don't worry if you pour more). Then tightly wrap the pork.

Insert the probe back into the meat through the foil, and return the pork to the smoker. At this point, no more smoke is being taken on, so you can continue to cook with just charcoal if you wish.

$\longrightarrow$

The Stall

When cooking brisket and pork shoulder, there is a point where the temperature almost seems to stop going up. It's this timeframe in which the meat is starting to rend fat at a higher rate. In so doing, the liquid from that rendering actually cools the meat, so that it is cooking but the rendering rate causes it to slow again. The internal temperature continues to rise at a faster rate since the fat has melted and the surrounding cells are warming up. That's why we wait for the meat to reach 165 degrees F when we wrap in aluminum foil or pink butcher paper, as that tends to be the sweet spot where the wrapping can enhance the stall but not lose the bark due to the wrapping.

Continue cooking wrapped until the internal temperature of the pork is between 200 and 203 degrees F. If you are using a digital Bluetooth thermometer, it is still important to double-check the temperature in a few different areas on the pork and look for a consistent temperature of 200 to 203 degrees F. When inserted, the probe should easily go in, like a knife inserted through room-temperature butter.

Remove the pork from the smoker, leaving it wrapped. Place it in a cooler that is not much bigger than the pork (with no ice), and let it rest for 1 hour. The cooler will keep the pork warm for hours, so if you are planning an event, better to be done early and let it sit. This resting time allows the moisture to get absorbed back into the pork.

Remove the pork from the cooler and begin pulling. Start by removing the bone (it should slide out cleanly), then pull with your favorite tool or with your hands. There will likely be some cartilage or other fatty pieces, so be sure to pull those out (it's not a good texture) and discard.

Serve and enjoy with your favorite sides and sauces.

We love this on a simple slider bun with a simple slaw with our Smoked Pickled Onions (page 122) and drizzled with our Honey Gold Sauce (page 63).

WINE PAIRING: Pork is such a versatile cut when pairing with wine. Without added sauce, it will be moist and slightly sweet and smoky. Consider a nice pinot noir or rosé. If you add sauce, follow our recommendation of the pairing based on the sauce. For vinegar-based sauces, high-acid white wines work well. For a Kansas City–style sauce, go for a bold, fruity wine like syrah or zinfandel.

Injecting Meat

Injecting can add flavor and moisture into a meat. Chicken, brisket, and pork shoulder are all great examples of cuts that can be injected using a large food syringe because, when smoking, you are cooking for a long time. Injecting helps prevent the meat from drying out, but it isn't required. It should be avoided for grilling. If we inject for pork, we typically use equal parts apple cider vinegar and apple juice. For beef we use beef broth, and for poultry we use chicken stock. You can mix a dry rub or other flavors into the liquids, so long as you have the right syringe that won't get clogged.

STUFFED PORK LOIN

We love a large stuffed pork loin to serve at a dinner party. One whole cut can run six to eight pounds or more. We get a smaller cut for an everyday family meal. You can prep everything in advance and place the loin on the grill an hour before dinner is planned. When it's done, all you have to do is slice and serve this hearty dish full of savory, earthy, and herbal flavors from the stuffing. Serve alongside roasted vegetables and potatoes and you've got our idea of a perfect Sunday meal with friends.

MAKES 6 SERVINGS

For the stuffing
1½ tablespoons extra-virgin olive oil, divided
3 pieces bacon, diced
8 ounces cremini mushrooms, diced
¾ cup diced red onions
2 cups tightly packed fresh spinach
2 cloves garlic, minced

¼ cup freshly grated Parmesan cheese
1 teaspoon chopped fresh thyme
½ teaspoon kosher salt
¼ teaspoon coarse ground black pepper

For the pork loin
1 (3½-pound) pork loin
1 tablespoon Poultry Rub (page 62)

Prepare the grill for direct/indirect cooking.

To make the stuffing, heat 1½ teaspoons of the oil in a large skillet over medium heat. Add the bacon and cook for 5 minutes, or until the bacon is crispy. Remove the bacon and set aside. Discard all but 1 tablespoon of the bacon grease.

To the same pan, add the mushrooms and onions and cook until soft, 6 to 8 minutes. Add the spinach and garlic and cook for 3 minutes, or until the spinach wilts. Stir in the Parmesan, thyme, salt, and pepper. Remove from the heat, mix in the bacon, and set aside.

To prepare the pork loin, follow the instructions on page 158 for butterflying a loin.

Follow the instructions on page 151 for rolling and tying a loin.

Coat the loin with the remaining 1 tablespoon oil, then season with the Poultry Rub.

Place the loin on the indirect side of the grill. The grill should read between 375 and 400 degrees F; adjust the dampeners as needed. Cook for 30 minutes covered, or until the internal temperature is 140 degrees F.

Remove from the grill and let sit for 10 minutes. Remove the string, slice into medallions, and serve.

WINE PAIRING: Choose a bold pinot noir or earthy cabernet franc (look for one from the Loire). If you want a white wine, try a barrel-fermented chardonnay.

Butterflying a Loin

When you have a large loin, a great way to create flavor is to butterfly the meat so you can open it like a trifold and have essentially a flat cut. To do this, you have to use a sharp knife.

Start by making a small cut at the base of the loin. Cut the loin with your knife parallel to the cutting board. Cut it horizontally one-third of the way from the bottom, stopping after 4 or 5 inches, depending on the size of loin. Then make another horizontal cut in the thicker part of the loin and continue slicing horizontal to cutting board until you have a flat piece of meat, another 4 to 5 inches. The final butterfly cut will be a large rectangle or square depending on size of the loin. Cover with plastic wrap, then use a meat hammer to flatten the loin evenly to about ½ inch thick.

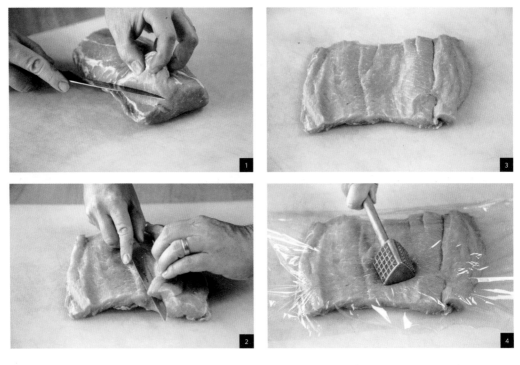

1 Slice the base of loin, but do not cut all the way through.
2 After opening the first third of the loin, cut again.
3 Open the loin like a trifold.
4 Place plastic wrap over the loin and pound out evenly.

Rolling and Tying a Loin

Spread the filling evenly on the cut side to within a ¼ inch of the edges. On one side of the loin, grab the two corners and roll up the loin tightly into a pinwheel. Using kitchen string, tie it together in at least three places (in the center and at the two outer edges).

1 Place the filling on one side of loin, leaving ½ inch along edges.
2 Tightly roll the loin.

3 Using kitchen string, tie along the entire length of the loin.
4 Loin should be secure, but not overly tight, and ready for the rub.

PORK BELLY BURNT ENDS

You've heard of brisket burnt ends—you know, those magical morsels of beef? But have you tried them with pork belly? This pork version is super tender, full of flavor, and easy to make.

When we first published a video for this recipe, it immediately went viral. To this day, it remains one of the most popular recipes on Vindulge.

People have clearly fallen in love with pork belly burnt ends. This technique has become a huge trend among BBQ nerds like us, and we affectionately call these sweet bits of charred goodness "meat candy." In this recipe, we cut the pork belly into cubes. This allows more surface area to smoke versus an entire belly, as well as speeds up the cooking.

MAKES 16 TO 20 SERVINGS, AS AN APPETIZER PORTION

5 pounds pork belly

3 tablespoons extra-virgin olive oil

1 cup Sweet Rub (page 62)

1 cup Pinot Noir BBQ Sauce (page 66)

3 tablespoons unsalted butter

2 tablespoons honey

Preheat the smoker to 225 degrees F using fruitwood (we like cherry for color and a sweeter flavor).

To prepare the pork belly, trim the excess skin and fat and slice into 2-inch cubes. Place the cubes in a large bowl, and coat liberally with the oil and Sweet Rub. Transfer the cubes to a wire rack or directly onto the smoker. The wire rack makes it easy to transport the cubes in and out of the smoker and allows the fat to not pool in a pan and drip into the smoker.

Smoke uncovered for 3 hours, or until a darker red color and a modest bark (or crust) develop.

Transfer the cubes to a 9-by-13-inch smoker-safe dish and add the Pinot Noir BBQ Sauce, butter, and honey. Stir. Cover the pan with aluminum foil and place it on the smoker. Cook for 90 minutes, or until the internal temperature of the meat is 200 to 203 degrees F. Remove the foil, stir, and smoke for another 15 minutes to let the sauce thicken. Remove from the smoker and serve immediately.

WINE PAIRING: The flavors here are big and bold. You've got the smoke, some richness, sweetness, and possibly spiciness from your BBQ sauce. You need a red wine that can handle that weight. We like a rich syrah, particularly from Washington State, for its deep fruit flavors and approachability.

GRILLED PORK TENDERLOIN MEDALLIONS WITH SAVORY APPLE BACON CHUTNEY

Inspired by beef tenderloin medallions, this pork tenderloin dish is a fun twist on the old-school pork and applesauce combination. The sweet and savory chutney for these small steaks of pork makes for a dramatic presentation. Our chutney of vinegar, fruit, and herbs works as a topping or base for the dish, and adds a more savory element versus the typical apple sauce.

MAKES 4 SERVINGS

For the pork tenderloin
  1 (1¼- to 1½-pound) pork tenderloin (look for the widest you can find)
  2 tablespoons extra-virgin olive oil,
  2 tablespoons Savory Rub (page 63)

For the chutney
  1½ teaspoons extra-virgin olive oil

  2 pieces bacon, finely diced
  ½ small red onion, finely diced
  ½ cup unsweetened applesauce, homemade if possible
  2 tablespoons apple cider vinegar
  1 tablespoon unsalted butter
  4 sage leaves, finely chopped
  Finishing salt

To prepare the tenderloin, cut off the thin tail at the end. Trim off the excess fat and remove the silverskin.

Cut the tenderloin into 8 equal pieces at least 1 inch thick. To ensure even cuts, it's best to cut the tenderloin in the center first. Take the two pieces and halve them, then repeat one more time. If your tenderloin is small, buy a second tenderloin and double the portions.

Coat the tenderloin medallions with the oil and the Savory Rub on all sides.

Prepare the grill for direct/indirect cooking. While the grill is coming to temperature, make the apple chutney.

To make the chutney, heat the oil in a medium skillet over medium heat and add the bacon. Stir until crispy, 8 to 10 minutes. Add the onions and cook for 5 minutes, or until translucent. Next, add the applesauce, vinegar, and butter. Let simmer for 6 minutes. Add the sage, remove from the heat, and set aside.

$\longrightarrow$

Place the tenderloins over direct heat for up to 3 minutes, or until you see a light crust develop. Flip the tenderloins and sear again over direct heat for another 3 minutes, or until you see a light crust develop. Move the tenderloins to the indirect side of the cooker, cover, and cook 8 to 10 minutes, or until the internal temperature of the thickest cut is at your desired doneness (we like 140 degrees F). Remove the tenderloins and let sit for 3 to 5 minutes.

Place a small amount of the chutney on each of four plates. Rest one or two tenderloins on it, then top with more of the chutney and a pinch of finishing salt.

WINE PAIRING: Try a New World fruity white wine. Fruity-style chardonnay, pinot gris, and riesling all work great with the sweet, herbal, and acidic chutney.

Anatomy of a Pig

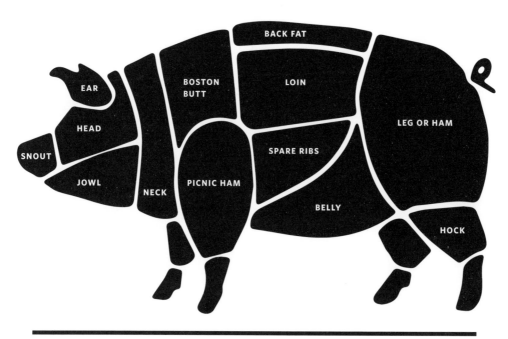

GRILLED PORK CHOPS WITH DRIED CHERRY RELISH

Who says pork chops and applesauce are the only great pork and fruit combination? Inspired by the bounty of living in Oregon's cherry country, we created this recipe to be made with fresh or dried cherries. If using dry, we like to rehydrate them with rosé wine to give them moisture and incredible flavor. This is going to be your new favorite pork chop recipe!

MAKES 4 SERVINGS; MAKES ABOUT ½ CUP RELISH

For the relish
- ½ cup dried or fresh cherries, chopped (see note)
- ⅓ cup rosé wine, or enough to cover the cherries
- 2 tablespoons finely chopped red bell pepper
- 1 tablespoon finely chopped shallots
- 1 tablespoon freshly squeezed orange juice
- 1 teaspoon finely chopped jalapeño pepper
- ¼ teaspoon orange zest

For the pork chops
- 4 (1½- to 2-inch-thick) bone-in pork chops
- 2 tablespoons extra-virgin olive oil
- 2 tablespoons Savory Rub (page 63)

To make the relish, put the cherries in a small bowl and cover with the wine. Soak for 1 hour. Drain, and discard the liquid.

In a medium bowl, combine the cherries, bell pepper, shallots, orange juice, jalapeño, and zest. Stir to combine and set aside.

Prepare the grill for direct/indirect cooking.

To prepare the pork chops, coat them with the oil and Savory Rub. Sear the chops over direct heat for 4 to 5 minutes, or until you see a nice crust form. Flip, and cook another 4 to 5 minutes. Move the chops to the indirect side and cover. Cook for 8 to 10 minutes, or until the chops are 140 degrees F. Let rest for 10 minutes.

Slice the chops along the bone to separate, then slice again perpendicular to the bone. Serve topped with the relish.

NOTE: If using fresh cherries, there's no need to soak them in wine, so skip the first step.

WINE PAIRING: Choose a fruity, light-bodied red wine with bright fruit, such as gamay, pinot noir, or Italian barbera. Stay away from earthy wines here.

THE ULTIMATE BLAT

Picture a warm evening in late summer, when tomatoes are at their best. Juicy, sweet, ripe tomatoes are meant to be eaten fresh, and they make for the perfect BLT. This one intensifies the greatness of a classic BLT with smoked thick-cut bacon, grilled avocado, and a delish homemade mayonnaise. It is truly out of this world! With the simplicity of such a dish, it's important to start with the freshest and best ingredients you can get your hands on.

MAKES 4 SANDWICHES

For the mayonnaise
- 1 tablespoon freshly squeezed lemon juice
- 1 egg yolk
- 2 cloves garlic, minced
- 1 teaspoon Dijon mustard
- 1 teaspoon white wine vinegar
- ½ cup avocado oil or other neutral-flavored oil
- ½ cup extra-virgin olive oil
- ¼ teaspoon kosher salt
- ¼ teaspoon Sweet Rub or your favorite pork rub or cayenne pepper

For the sandwich
- 8 pieces thick-cut bacon
- 2 avocados, sliced in half lengthwise and pit removed
- Sourdough bread loaf or your favorite bread loaf, cut into 8 slices
- 1 head butter lettuce
- 2 large fresh heirloom or beefsteak tomatoes, sliced thick
- Finishing salt

Prepare the grill for direct/indirect cooking with a target range of 375 to 400 degrees F. As the grill is coming to temperature, make the mayonnaise.

To make the mayonnaise, add the lemon juice, egg yolk, garlic, Dijon, and vinegar in a medium bowl. Whisk quickly for at least 30 seconds to combine. Very slowly add a small amount of the oil while continuing to whisk vigorously. Gradually add the rest of the oil, in a very slow and thin stream, whisking while the mayonnaise thickens. The whole process should take 4 to 5 minutes, and the end result should look pale yellow and thick. Stir in the salt and Sweet Rub. Taste and adjust as desired.

Prepare the sandwich elements. On the indirect side of the grill, lay out the bacon perpendicular to the grates so they don't fall through. Cover and cook the bacon 12 to 14 minutes, or until crispy. The time is going to vary based on the size of your grill. Cooking indirect prevents flare-ups from grease. If your grill space is small, rotate the bacon between the direct and indirect sides. The key is firm, crispy bacon. Remove and set aside.

As the bacon finishes, grill the avocado. Place the avocado flesh side down over direct heat for no more than 3 minutes. Flip to the skin side for another 3 minutes to let the avocado soften. Remove, slice, and set aside.

Place the slices of bread over direct heat and cook for no more than 2 minutes per side. You are looking for a slight toast.

Construct the sandwich with a layer of mayo on the bread, then two pieces of lettuce, two slices of tomato, slices from a grilled avocado half, two pieces of bacon, and more mayo. Sprinkle finishing salt to taste and then top with bread.

WINE PAIRING: To us, this sandwich is the perfect excuse to pop open a bright, fruity rosé with zesty acidity. Sparkling rosé will work even better, cutting perfectly through the creamy mayo and grilled avocado. If you're itching for red, a fruity Beaujolais (made from gamay) will ease the craving.

LAMB JAM

There's something magical that happens when you cook lamb over wood fire. The smoke tends to tame some of the gamy flavors from this protein, and a mix of sweet and earthy flavors emerge. From ground lamb to a dramatic crown roast, there are incredible things that await with this flavorful meat.

Adding a little contrast to the lamb flavor is another great way to make lamb shine. We do this with an orange glaze or a mint salsa verde. The key with lamb is getting it as fresh as possible. That gamy flavor gets more intense the longer the time from when the lamb was processed. Marbling, like steak, is another item to keep an eye out for. The intramuscular fat flavors the meat and is important when selecting your cuts.

GRILLED LAMB STEAKS WITH SALSA VERDE

Neither of us grew up eating much lamb. It wasn't until Mary was in her late twenties that she even tried it for the first time, and she was admittedly a bit nervous. But, hot damn, she was an instant fan. Think of this cut as being similar to a pork chop or rib-eye steak but with a delicate texture and sweet taste. Grilling brings down any gaminess of the lamb, and the salsa verde topping makes a fantastic complement to the flavors of the meat. The salsa verde is comparable to a chimichurri sauce but with a little kick and a greater amount of bright herbs.

MAKES 4 SERVINGS

For the salsa verde
- 2 cups fresh Italian parsley, stems removed
- 2 tablespoons freshly squeezed lemon juice
- 2 tablespoons apple cider vinegar
- 2 tablespoons chopped shallots (about 1 small shallot)
- ½ medium jalapeño pepper, seeds and membrane removed, chopped (1 tablespoon)
- 1 tablespoon chopped fresh mint
- 2 cloves garlic, crushed
- 1 teaspoon capers
- 1 teaspoon chopped fresh oregano
- ¼ teaspoon kosher salt
- ½ cup extra-virgin olive oil

For the lamb
- 4 (½-pound) lamb steaks
- 2 teaspoons extra-virgin olive oil
- 2 teaspoons Savory Rub (page 63)

To make the salsa verde, put the parsley, lemon juice, vinegar, shallots, jalapeño, mint, garlic, capers, oregano, and salt in a food processor and pulse a few times to combine. Slowly drizzle in the oil and continue pulsing, until the sauce is well chopped but not pureed.

To make the lamb, prepare the grill for direct cooking.

Coat each lamb steak with ½ teaspoon of the oil, then apply ½ teaspoon of the Savory Rub to each steak on both sides.

Cook the lamb over direct heat for 5 minutes. Flip and cook for another 5 minutes, or until the temperature reads 135 degrees F on an instant-read thermometer. Remove from the heat and let rest for 10 minutes. Drizzle the salsa verde over each lamb steak.

WINE PAIRING: The delicate flavor of the lamb shines here and is accented by the fresh herb salsa. Avoid powerful and rich wines for this dish. A bolder pinot noir is a fantastic match. Southern Rhône reds and sangiovese also work well.

SMOKED CROWN LAMB ROAST

A crown lamb roast makes for an incredibly festive centerpiece for any holiday or special occasion. It's also easy to slice into equal portions for your guests, and nobody is left fighting for a bone piece (they all get one). This impressive display is formed by connecting two lamb rib racks (usually with eight bones each), tied together. The racks usually come with fat to the end of the bone, so ask your butcher to french them, as this can be a challenge to do yourself. Let the butcher know you're making a crown roast and he or she will know what to do.

Instead of stuffing the crown roast before cooking (as many recipes will have you do), roast some root vegetables or potatoes on the side and stuff them in the hollow opening of the roast just before serving.

MAKES 6 TO 8 SERVINGS

For the herb paste
- 1 cup fresh parsley, stems removed
- 3 tablespoons roughly chopped shallots
- 2 tablespoons roughly chopped fresh sage
- 2 tablespoons freshly squeezed lemon juice
- 1 tablespoon roughly chopped fresh oregano
- 1 tablespoon roughly chopped fresh thyme
- 1½ teaspoons chopped fresh rosemary
- 1 teaspoon roughly chopped garlic
- ½ teaspoon kosher salt
- ½ cup extra-virgin olive oil

For the lamb
- 2 racks of lamb, frenched (8 bones each)
- 1½ teaspoons extra-virgin olive oil

Special tool
- Cooking twine

To make the herb paste, put the parsley, shallots, sage, lemon juice, oregano, thyme, rosemary, garlic, and salt in a food processor. Pulse twice. Turn the processor on and slowly add the oil. Continue to process for 1 minute. Using a spatula, scrape down the sides of the bowl and process again for 1 minute.

To make the lamb, trim any excess fat, then apply the herb paste liberally to both racks.

Preheat the smoker to 225 degrees F using cherrywood or applewood.

Next, construct a crown following the instructions on page 167. Create a circle with the two racks with the bones facing up and the meat facing inside the circle. To tie the roast, wrap the entire roast with cooking twine where the flesh meets the exposed bone and tighten slightly. Repeat this at the base of the rib and tighten. Place on a baking sheet.

Transfer the roast from the baking sheet to the grill and insert a meat probe. Smoke for 90 minutes, or until the internal temperature is 130 degrees F.

$\longrightarrow$

Set the grill for direct grilling or use a large cast-iron skillet on the stove over high heat to sear. Cook over direct heat until the temperature of the lamb reaches 135 to 140 degrees F.

Remove the roast from the smoker and place on your serving tray. If you have roasted any veggies or potatoes, stuff them inside the roast. Slice and serve at the table after resting 15 minutes.

WINE PAIRING: This is an elegant meal, and the meat is super tender and full of flavor. Syrah is a favorite here, ideally from Washington State or northern Rhône. A bold pinot noir or cabernet franc works too, especially one with an earthy or herbal style.

How to Construct a Crown Roast

1. Tie kitchen twine onto a skewer and thread between the top of the first and second bone.
2. Pull the twine through and align the other rib rack directly next to it.
3. On the second rib rack, thread the twine through the top of the first and second rib.
4. Pull the twine through. Optional: repeat the same steps for the bottom portion of the rib.
5. Tie a double knot tightly so that the two ribs are held closely together.
6. Cut off the free side of the twine. The other side should remain intact.
7. Bring twine along the frenched side of the ribs and use skewer to punch through the first and second rib.
8. Align racks and thread the skewer through the other rack between the first and second bone. Tie it off.

WINE-BRAISED SMOKED LAMB SHANKS

Braised lamb shanks make for such an elegant winter meal. By smoking the lamb first for a few hours, you're imparting incredible flavor to the final dish. Finish the lamb in a stockpot filled with earthy vegetables, red wine, beef stock, and herbs, and you've got yourself an exquisite meal for a dinner party or date night at home.

MAKES 4 TO 6 SERVINGS

4 lamb shanks

3 tablespoons extra-virgin olive oil, divided

2 tablespoons Beef Rub (page 63)

½ cup diced yellow onion

½ cup diced carrots

½ cup diced celery

2 cloves garlic, chopped

1 cup dry red wine

3 cups beef stock

1 large rosemary sprig

1 tablespoon tomato paste

1 bay leaf

Preheat the smoker to 225 degrees F using cherrywood or applewood.

Coat each lamb shank with 1½ teaspoons of the oil and season each with 1½ teaspoons of the Beef Rub.

Place the shanks on the smoker and cook until the internal temperature is 165 degrees F. This will take 90 minutes to 2 hours, depending on the shank size. Remove the shanks from the smoker.

Meanwhile, in a large saucepan over medium heat, add the remaining 1 tablespoon oil, the onions, carrots, and celery and sauté for 8 minutes, or until the vegetables are soft (but not caramelized). Add the garlic and cook for 2 minutes.

Add the shanks and wine, and bring the wine to a simmer. Add the beef stock, rosemary, tomato paste, and bay leaf. Bring back to a simmer, then cover and let simmer at the lowest heat for another 2 hours, or until the shanks are fork-tender. Serve over a creamy root vegetable puree or creamy polenta or with some crusty bread to soak up the juices.

WINE PAIRING: This richly flavored and earthy dish works wonders with a New World cabernet franc, syrah, malbec, tempranillo from Ribera del Duero, or a hearty, earthy Old World wine such as a Rhône blend or young Bordeaux red.

LAMB MEATBALLS WITH ORANGE MARMALADE

We created this recipe to pair with an orange-style wine, in this case riesling. It had an interesting mix of earthy and orange flavors which we incorporated into the glaze for these meatballs. This is a really cool pairing for a unique wine and flavorful lamb.

MAKES 12 TO 14 MEATBALLS

For the meatballs

1 pound ground lamb, 80 percent lean/
20 percent fat or 85 percent lean/
15 percent fat

¼ cup diced white onion

1 egg, beaten

1 teaspoon minced garlic

½ teaspoon smoked paprika

½ teaspoon kosher salt

½ teaspoon coarse ground black pepper

¼ teaspoon red chili pepper flakes

¼ teaspoon cumin

For the marmalade

1 (12-ounce) jar orange marmalade (some
European jars are 13 ounces)

¼ cup apple cider vinegar

¼ teaspoon crushed red chili pepper flakes

¼ teaspoon kosher salt

To make the meatballs, preheat the smoker to 225 degrees F using applewood or cherrywood.

In a large bowl, combine the lamb, onion, egg, garlic, paprika, salt, black pepper, pepper flakes, and cumin. Mix gently with your hands until the ingredients are incorporated.

Roll the mixture into golf ball–size meatballs (about 1 tablespoon) and place them on a baking sheet.

Put the baking sheet on the smoker for up to 1 hour, or until the meatballs come to an internal temperature of 160 degrees F. Once the meatballs are done smoking, make the marmalade.

To make the marmalade, combine the jarred marmalade, vinegar, pepper flakes, and salt in a medium saucepan over low heat and bring to a simmer. Cook for 8 minutes. Add the meatballs, and let simmer for an additional 10 minutes.

Remove the meatballs from the marmalade and enjoy.

WINE PAIRING: Funky flavors call for a funky wine. We find this recipe fascinating with a slightly oxidized wine, which can add richness and umami characteristics. Sherry and Madeira are examples of oxidized wines, as are wines from the Jura region of France. Another interesting choice is an orange-style wine (a white wine made similar to a red wine, fermented with skin contact so it turns amber).

LAMB RAGÙ

This is our take on a classic beef dish. We start with ground lamb, smoke for additional flavor, then use that as the base for this superrich and thick ragù. The texture is divine, and the slow simmer incorporates the red sauce into the meat, making this dish a great pairing with wine.

MAKES 4 TO 6 SERVINGS

1 pound ground lamb
1 tablespoon extra virgin olive oil
½ cup diced celery
½ cup diced red onion
½ cup diced carrot
2 cloves garlic, minced
½ cup dry red wine
1 (28-ounce) can whole San Marzano tomatoes
½ cup chicken stock

1 tablespoon tomato paste
1 teaspoon kosher salt
½ teaspoon dried fennel
½ teaspoon ground coriander
½ teaspoon chopped fresh rosemary
½ teaspoon coarse ground black pepper
8 fresh basil leaves, chopped
1 pound pasta, such as pappardelle, rigatoni, or penne
½ cup shredded Parmesan cheese

Preheat the smoker to 225 degrees F using cherrywood.

Break up the lamb into smaller chunks, place them on a baking sheet, and then into the smoker. Smoke for 45 minutes, then remove and set aside.

In a large saucepan over medium heat, heat the oil. Add the celery, onions, and carrots. Sauté for 8 minutes, or until the vegetables are soft and translucent. Add the garlic and cook 1 minute.

Add the wine and simmer for 4 to 5 minutes to reduce. Add the tomatoes, chicken stock, tomato paste, salt, fennel, coriander, rosemary, pepper, and lamb. Stir to combine.

Cover and simmer on low for 2 hours, until reduced.

When the ragù is almost done, cook the pasta according to package directions.

Remove the ragù from the heat and stir in the basil.

Serve the ragù with the pasta, topped with the Parmesan.

WINE PAIRING: This rich and hearty pasta dish shines with Chianti (or other sangiovese), barbera, Bordeaux blends, Rhône-style blends, and even fuller-bodied pinot noirs.

LAMB BURGERS

Ground lamb makes for an incredible base for a great burger. Ditch the traditional Greek-style burger filled with feta, cucumbers, and tzatziki, which frankly mask the flavors of that delicious meat. Instead, season simply and top with an easy horseradish-and-ketchup mayonnaise. Let those authentic flavors of the lamb shine through.

MAKES 4 BURGERS

1¼ pounds ground lamb 80 percent lean/20 percent fat

2 tablespoons Worcestershire sauce

1 tablespoon Poultry Rub (page 62)

1 tablespoon plus 1 teaspoon horseradish, divided

4 slices provolone cheese

4 soft brioche buns

½ cup ketchup

¼ cup mayonnaise

1 head butter lettuce

½ cup Smoked Pickled Onions (page 122)

Prepare the grill for direct/indirect cooking.

In a large bowl, combine the lamb, Worcestershire sauce, Poultry Rub, and 1 teaspoon of the horseradish. Mix with your hands to incorporate. Divide into 4 portions and shape into burgers. The burgers shrink while they cook, so we strive for a little more than ¼ pound precooked weight per burger. Grill, covered, 6 to 7 minutes over direct heat. Flip, cover, and cook another 6 to 7 minutes. Move the burgers to indirect heat. The temperature of the patty should range from 100 to 120 degrees F on an instant-read thermometer at this point. You want a nice sear but not a burned patty when moving it to the indirect heat.

Cook until the internal temperature of the meat is 150 degrees F. Top each burger with a slice of cheese and cook 8 minutes, or until the internal temperature is 160 degrees F and the cheese is melted.

Remove from the heat and let sit for 10 minutes while toasting the buns. Place the buns on the grill over direct heat, cut side down, for 2 minutes, or until a nice light toast appears.

Meanwhile, make the sauce. In a small bowl, combine the ketchup, mayonnaise, and the remaining 1 tablespoon horseradish. This sauce is delicious on french fries as well.

Construct the burgers. On the bottom bun, layer the lettuce, patty, sauce, Smoked Pickled Onions, and top bun.

WINE PAIRING: Grenache, mourvedre, pinot noir, or even a juicy syrah all work wonders with this equally juicy and tender burger.

FROM THE RIVERS TO THE SEA: FISH AND SEAFOOD

We could probably write an entire book on the bounty of the sea and rivers of the Pacific Northwest and wood-fired food. It all starts with the fish. Trout and salmon have been smoked and served here for millennia. Whitefish (trout, sea bass, halibut, cod) take to smoke really well, and they grill fast over direct heat. Adding smoke to salmon just brings out more of the rich flavor.

Dungeness crab pots can be seen in the early part of our year, making fresh crab plentiful. Grilled crab cakes make an easy and flavorful dish as a meal or an appetizer. Scallops are also widely available and have such a rich, buttery character. They are perfect for a hot and fast cook.

When sourcing seafood, we go with line-caught fish or seafood that isn't farmed. With farmed fish, you may get fattier texture, which is good for smoking, but you don't get that taste of the sea. We encourage you to consider wild-caught fish as often as you can for best results, but recognize some fish like trout are often farm raised.

GRILLED SCALLOPS WITH HONEY BUTTER

Look for diver scallops, referred to as dry or day boat scallops, which are harvested by hand right from the sea and should smell like the ocean. They aren't treated with any chemicals, unlike wet scallops, which are treated with a phosphate solution and water to extend their life. Wet scallops absorb some of that water, plumping them up and as a result reducing the pure flavors. Diver scallops should have a sweeter and more natural flavor. The only downside is they don't stay fresh long, so they're best cooked soon after purchasing.

They are ridiculously delicious grilled and tossed in our sweet Smoked Honey Butter.

MAKES 2 SERVINGS

1 pound jumbo sea scallops (ideally, diver scallops), rinsed and patted dry

1 tablespoon Sweet Rub (page 62)

2 tablespoons Smoked Honey Butter (recipe follows)

Pinch of finishing salt

Prepare the grill for direct/indirect cooking.

Season the scallops liberally with the Sweet Rub on both sides.

Grill over direct heat (consider using a plancha or cast-iron pan if the scallops are small) for 3 to 4 minutes, flip, and cook for another 3 to 4 minutes, or until the internal temperature of a scallop is 130 degrees F. Remove from the grill.

Meanwhile, in a small cast-iron skillet on the coolest part of the grill, heat the Smoked Honey Butter until just melted.

Place the scallops on a serving dish, drizzle with Smoked Honey Butter, and sprinkle with the salt.

WINE PAIRING: Scallops work well with a medium- to full-bodied white or with a high-acid wine that will counterbalance the richness. Chardonnays of all kinds (whether oaked or crisp and fruity) are great matches for these scallops. Sparkling wine also works fantastically as well. Other alternatives include chenin blanc, albariño, or even off-dry riesling. Avoid red wines with this dish because most will overpower the flavors of the sweet scallops and butter sauce.

Smoked Honey Butter

A crowd pleaser at many of our events, smoked honey butter is an easy infusion of smoke into the honey, which is then whisked with butter. It's great as a base for a sauce or as a spread for bread topped with finishing salt. Because honey comes in various jar sizes, we have learned a rough ratio is to use two-thirds the butter to the honey. For example, for a sixteen-ounce jar of honey, add eleven ounces of butter. For a twelve-ounce jar, use eight ounces of butter. You can roll and freeze the honey butter for use throughout the year.

MAKES 2½ CUPS

1 (12-ounce) jar local honey

8 ounces unsalted butter, at room temperature

Pinch of finishing salt

Preheat the smoker to 200 degrees F using applewood or cherrywood.

Put the honey in a smoker-safe dish (we use a small glass dish) and place on the smoker for 3 hours.

Remove from the smoker, and allow the honey to come to room temperature.

In the bowl of a stand mixer, combine the butter and honey and mix on high speed until whipped, about 3 minutes. It comes together quickly.

Transfer to a serving container and top with finishing salt.

NOTE: It is important to keep the smoker under 212 degrees F and avoid boiling the honey. You want to see steam rising. It is also important to allow the honey to come to room temperature before whipping; otherwise, the butter will melt and the texture will be more liquid than whipped. Some honey is thicker than others. If you find the honey is not easily pouring into your smoker-safe dish, mix 2 tablespoons of water with the honey to thin it out. We have put as much as ¼ cup of water in 12 ounces of honey, depending on the consistency.

GRILLED WHOLE TROUT

Trout, which is readily available in the Pacific Northwest, has a light texture and mild flavor. It doesn't require much to enhance its flavor, so when we grill it, we love to do the whole fish. Stuff the trout with aromatic herbs to add distinct flavors.

MAKES 4 TO 6 SERVINGS

4 (1½- to 2-pound) whole trout, gutted, rinsed, and dried

2 tablespoons extra-virgin olive oil

2 tablespoons Savory Rub (page 63)

2 lemons (1 sliced thin, 1 cut in half for grilling)

4 large sprigs fresh rosemary

8 large sprigs fresh thyme

½ red onion, thinly sliced

¾ teaspoon capers, chopped

Pinch of finishing salt

Prepare the grill for direct/indirect cooking.

If your trout are large, they may need to be scaled. To do so, place your hand on the tail. Using the blade side of a fillet knife, scrape the fish from tail to head in one direction a few times. Do this on both sides of the fish.

Next, crosshatch the trout using an X scoring pattern twice on the skin side of each fish. This simply means you cut slightly through the skin and into the flesh, not deeply, to allow seasoning and smoke to better permeate the flesh.

Coat the outside of each trout with 1½ teaspoons of the oil.

Season the trout from the inside out, using 1½ teaspoons of the Savory Rub per fish. Start with a light coating of rub in the fish cavity, and then season both sides.

Stuff the cavity of each trout with 2 or 3 lemon slices, 1 rosemary sprig, 2 thyme sprigs, and a few slices of onion. Don't be afraid to jam these in the cavity.

Using butcher's twine, tie the fish closed in two places to keep the stuffing intact when flipping on the grill.

Grill the trout, covered, for up to 7 minutes per side. The fillets are small and will cook quickly on each side. If you have flare-ups, move the trout to the indirect side after a quick sear and cover.

Remove the trout from the grill when the internal temperature of the fish is 130 degrees F. While the trout are still warm, squeeze fresh lemon juice and scatter the capers over the fish, then sprinkle a pinch of finishing salt.

NOTE: To grill lemons, cut in half through the middle and grill over direct heat for 6 to 7 minutes, or until desired char marks appear.

WINE PAIRING: Fruity, bright acidic whites pair well with this lively dish. Pinot blanc, albariño, and chenin blanc all work nicely too.

GRILLED CRAB CAKES

A good crab cake is one of our favorite treats in the world. Grilling is a fantastic way to maintain the integrity of that tender, sweet crab meat, while intensifying the flavor. You can grill directly on the grill grates, but they need to be very clean and well oiled. We prefer to cook them in a cast-iron skillet heated over a charcoal grill, which cooks the crab cakes while also imparting some smoke flavor.

With crab, you get what you pay for, so make sure you're ready to splurge on the good stuff. It's so worth it!

MAKES 4 SERVINGS

1 pound Dungeness crab, lump meat, precooked

½ cup panko bread crumbs

¼ cup chopped shallots

¼ teaspoon red chili pepper flakes

2 tablespoons crème fraîche

1 clove garlic, finely minced

1 egg

1 teaspoon Sweet Rub (page 62)

Extra-virgin olive oil, for the pan

In a large bowl, combine the crab, bread crumbs, shallots, pepper flakes, crème fraîche, garlic, egg, and Sweet Rub. Form the mixture into 2½-inch patties about ½ inch thick. Refrigerate for 1 hour.

Prepare the grill for direct/indirect grilling.

Place a cast-iron skillet over direct heat and add oil to coat. Allow the pan and oil to warm for a few minutes.

Add the crab cakes gently; you should hear a sizzle. Cook the crab cakes for 3 to 4 minutes, then flip. Cook for another 3 to 4 minutes, or until golden brown.

Remove and serve with your favorite dipping sauce. We like our Basic Aioli (page 69).

WINE PAIRING: Reach for sparkling wines with crab cakes. There's nothing better for the delicate, sweet flavors of the Dungeness crab, and the bubbles cut through the richness and crunchy outer textures of the cakes. You can splurge and go big with Champagne (yes, please!) or go easy with Cava or a domestic blanc de blancs–style bubbly. Pinot blanc also works quite nicely, as does albariño.

GRILLED COD TACOS

Tacos are something we enjoy with our kids several times a week! It's one of the most crowd-friendly meals on the planet. For fish tacos, cod is our go-to affordable cut that easily marinates. Take the grill flavor, then add the texture of the slaw and the bright flavor of a crema, and you have our go-to grilled cod tacos—picky kid approved! Make some Grilled Mixed Pepper Salsa Verde (page 85) to serve with chips.

MAKES 10 TO 12 TACOS (OR 5 TO 6 SERVINGS)

For the marinade
- ¼ cup extra-virgin olive oil
- ¼ cup freshly squeezed lemon juice (or the juice of 1 large lemon)
- 2 tablespoons chopped red onion
- 1½ teaspoons Sweet Rub (page 62)
- 1½ teaspoons honey
- 1 clove garlic, minced

For the cod
- 1½ pounds fresh cod fillet (2 full fillets)
- 2 tablespoons Sweet Rub (page 62)

For the slaw
- 1 cup shredded red cabbage
- 1 cup shredded savoy cabbage
- ¼ cup shredded red onion
- ¼ cup shredded carrot
- 1 tablespoon chopped jalapeño pepper
- ⅛ teaspoon kosher salt
- ⅛ scant teaspoon freshly ground black pepper
- 1 tablespoon apple cider vinegar
- 1 teaspoon freshly squeezed lime juice

For the crema
- ¼ cup sour cream
- ¼ cup mayonnaise
- 1 clove garlic, minced
- 2 teaspoons hot sauce
- 1 teaspoon Sweet Rub (page 62)
- 1 teaspoon freshly squeezed lime juice
- 10 to 12 corn tortillas
- Chopped cilantro, for garnish
- Lime wedges, for garnish

To make the marinade, in a 1-gallon ziplock bag, combine the oil, lemon juice, onion, Sweet Rub, honey, and garlic. Seal the bag and shake the ingredients to combine. Open the bag and add the cod fillets.

Seal the bag, taking care to remove as much air from the bag as possible. Marinate in the refrigerator for no more than 2 hours. If it marinates any longer, the fish may cook due to the acid from the lemon juice.

To make the slaw, in a large bowl, add the cabbages, onion, carrot, jalapeño, salt, pepper, vinegar, and lime juice. Mix together. This can be made in advance and stored in the refrigerator for up to 3 days.

To make the crema, in a medium bowl, combine the sour cream, mayonnaise, garlic, hot sauce, Sweet Rub, and lime juice and mix well. This can be made in advance and stored in the refrigerator for up to 3 days.

Prepare the grill for direct cooking.

To prepare the cod, remove it from the marinade and discard the marinade. Pat the cod dry with a paper towel, then season each fillet with 1 tablespoon of the Sweet Rub, making sure to apply it to both sides.

When the charcoal is evenly lit, place the cod over direct heat for 4 to 5 minutes, then flip. (It is easiest to use a large spatula versus tongs as the cod will be delicate when flipping. It will likely come apart, which is fine.) Cook for another 4 to 5 minutes, or until the internal temperature is 135 degrees F. It will temp up to 140 degrees F.

Remove the cod from the grill and let sit for 5 minutes, then break up into chunks for the tacos.

To construct the tacos, warm the tortillas. On each tortilla, layer the cod, slaw, crema, and cilantro. Squeeze fresh lime juice from the wedges and enjoy.

WINE PAIRING: This preparation is one of our favorite weeknight summer meals, though it can certainly be enjoyed year-round. The fresh, bright flavors of the fish are fantastic with a fruity and crisp albariño. Rosé comes a close second, followed by Napa sauvignon blanc (which tends to have a nice balance of fruity and citrus flavors), and a fruity pinot gris/grigio. For the kiddos, nothing beats a cold glass of lemonade with these bright tacos.

MAPLE-CHIPOTLE CEDAR PLANK GRILLED SALMON

Cedar plank salmon is amazing when coated with a sweet and spicy dry rub, cooked on the grill to give it that smoked influence, and finished with a maple syrup glaze. Sweet, spicy, and absolutely incredible.

When using a cedar plank, soak it in water, place the fish on top, and then lay the plank over direct or indirect heat. This allows for the plank's flavor to infuse the food.

MAKES 4 TO 6 SERVINGS

For the dry rub
- 2 tablespoons brown sugar
- 1 tablespoon chili powder
- 1½ teaspoons cumin
- 1 teaspoon dried chipotle powder
- 1 teaspoon kosher salt
- ½ teaspoon freshly ground black pepper

For the salmon
- 1½ pounds wild-caught salmon (we like coho)
- 1 tablespoon extra-virgin olive oil
- 2 tablespoons maple syrup

Special tool
- 1 cedar plank

Soak the cedar plank, fully submerged in water, for 30 minutes. Pat dry after removing from the water.

Prepare the grill for indirect cooking.

To make the dry rub, in a small bowl, combine the brown sugar, chili powder, cumin, chipotle powder, salt, and pepper.

To prepare the salmon, coat the salmon with the oil, then sprinkle about 2 tablespoons of the dry rub liberally over it (you may have some dry rub left over depending on the size of your salmon).

Place the salmon on the cedar plank, and put it on direct heat for up to 15 minutes, or until the salmon reaches an internal temperature of 120 degrees F.

Transfer the salmon and plank to indirect heat. Using a silicone brush, glaze the salmon with the maple syrup. Remove after 1 minute.

Let rest for 5 minutes, then slice and serve.

WINE PAIRING: Riesling provides a refreshing and sweet contrast to the spicy chipotle flavors. It will also balance the sweetness of the dry rub and maple syrup. For red wine, go for a medium-bodied fruity pinot noir from California.

GRILLED HALIBUT WITH ROASTED HAZELNUT CRUST

Halibut from off the coast of Oregon is truly amazing. This whitefish absorbs so much flavor when cooked over a grill that you need to be careful not to overseason it. For example, halibut cooked on a cedar plank will suck in that cedar flavor, and you'll lose the tender, delicate taste that naturally exists in the fish. So we find that cooking on a direct grill and using a mild seasoning to add texture preserve the authenticity of the halibut while still offering a slight taste from the grill. Inspired by Northwest hazelnuts, this dish is something we enjoy often over the summer.

MAKES 4 SERVINGS

½ cup raw hazelnuts

¼ cup panko bread crumbs

¾ teaspoon kosher salt

½ teaspoon coarse ground black pepper

½ teaspoon chopped fresh thyme

1 pound halibut fillet or steaks, preferably thick

1 tablespoon extra-virgin olive oil

In a small cast-iron skillet or sauté pan over medium-high heat, toast the hazelnuts for 4 minutes, or until you smell a roasted aroma. (Alternatively, you could toast the hazelnuts on the grill.) Be sure to consistently move the nuts around to avoid scorching.

Put the warm nuts in a food processor and pulse to a fine texture like grainy salt.

In a medium bowl, add the hazelnuts, bread crumbs, salt, pepper, and thyme, and mix with a spoon. This can be made in advance and stored in an airtight container.

Prepare the grill for direct/indirect cooking with a target temperature in the grill of 400 degrees F.

Coat both sides of the halibut with the oil and season with the hazelnut mixture on the flesh side only.

Place the halibut on the grill skin side down over direct heat and cover. Cook for 8 to 10 minutes, or until the internal temperature of the halibut is 135 degrees F. The cooking time will depend on the thickness of the halibut. Do not flip the halibut; the skin will act as a protective layer between the flame and the meat. You will see a slight browning of the hazelnut mixture. If you have grill flare-ups, move the halibut to the indirect side to finish.

WINE PAIRING: This grilled halibut is fresh and pure with slight nuttiness from the toasted hazelnut crust. We love this with an Italian arneis, Oregon pinot gris, Chablis (or other low- to no-oak chardonnay), or even blanc de blancs Champagne.

SMOKED WHITEFISH CHOWDER

Adding a bit of smoke to a dish like chowder is a great way to enhance flavor. Here we smoke the fish to get a little kick. We tend to stick with mild woods when smoking foods, but this one is an exception. Mesquite will infuse the fish with a much-needed smokiness to help intensify the flavors of the chowder—made even more flavorful by that Smoked Chicken Stock (page 94) you have in your freezer from your last roaster chicken, and you have an easy and delicious chowder. We use whitefish because it is mild in flavor and blends in with the color of the chowder.

MAKES 3 QUARTS (8 SERVINGS)

1 pound sea bass (cod or halibut are also great choices)

1 teaspoon extra-virgin olive oil

2 teaspoons Savory Rub (page 63)

2 tablespoons unsalted butter

¼ pound finely diced thick-cut bacon (4 slices)

1 cup finely diced celery

½ cup finely diced carrot

1½ cups rinsed and finely diced leeks, white and pale green parts only

⅓ cup all-purpose flour

3½ cups whole milk

2½ cups Smoked Chicken Stock (page 94), or store-bought chicken stock

1 bay leaf

1½ pounds diced Yukon gold potatoes

¾ cup crème fraîche

1 tablespoon freshly squeezed lemon juice

2 teaspoons kosher salt, plus more to taste

Preheat the smoker to 225 degrees F using mesquite or hickory wood. Mesquite will lend a smokier taste to the soup versus a milder fruitwood.

Season the fish with the oil and Savory Rub, then place it on the smoker for 30 to 45 minutes, or until the internal temperature is 140 degrees F.

In a large stockpot over medium heat, melt the butter and cook the bacon for 6 minutes, or until it is browned.

Add the celery and carrots and sauté until tender, about 4 minutes.

Add the leeks and cook for 2 to 3 minutes. Gradually add the flour and cook 1 to 2 minutes, stirring constantly.

Whisk in the milk and Smoked Chicken Stock. Add the bay leaf and stir until the mixture comes to a simmer, about 8 minutes.

Add the potatoes, cover, and simmer over low heat, stirring frequently to make sure the

$\longrightarrow$

milk doesn't on scorch the bottom. A metal fish spatula works great to scrape the bottom and it gets into the corners of the pot.

After 30 minutes, check the potatoes for tenderness. Add the smoked fish, crème fraîche, lemon juice, and salt. Taste and add more salt if desired.

Remove from the heat and stir to incorporate.

Serve with croutons or oyster crackers, fresh cracked black pepper, and fresh watercress dressed with fresh lemon juice.

WINE PAIRING: Chowder is rich, and this one has sweet and smoky fish integrated into the flavors. This is made for a full-bodied chardonnay to match the weight of the dish. Viognier, Rhône-style white blends, or other full-bodied whites work wonders too.

PERFECT SMOKED SALMON FILLET WITH BEURRE BLANC

Salmon is a Northwest specialty, where it has been smoked for millennia. We serve our salmon medium rare to keep the moisture of the fish while preserving its wild flavor.

We served this exact dish at a seventy-five-person wine dinner at Anne Amie Vineyards. Guests were blown away by the flavor, and we received endless requests for the recipe. The secret comes from simply buying the freshest wild-caught salmon and not overcooking the quality fish. The beurre blanc may sound fancy, but it's quite simple to make and is the icing on the cake for this flavorful meal and beautiful presentation.

MAKES 6 TO 8 SERVINGS

For the salmon

1 (2½-pound) wild-caught salmon fillet (we like coho)

1½ teaspoons extra-virgin olive oil

1½ teaspoons kosher salt

1½ teaspoons coarse ground black pepper

For the beurre blanc

8 tablespoons unsalted butter, cut into 8 equal pieces

2 tablespoons minced shallots

¼ cup chardonnay or other full-bodied white wine

2 tablespoons white wine vinegar

1 teaspoon chopped fresh tarragon

¼ teaspoon kosher salt

Preheat the smoker to 225 degrees F using alderwood, applewood, or cherrywood.

To prepare the salmon, pat the salmon dry. Using tweezers, remove the pin bones. We like to make small slices along the fillet, not going through the skin, to precut serving sizes and get a little more smoke and rub into the salmon.

Coat the salmon with the oil and apply the salt and pepper.

Place the salmon on the smoker, skin side down, for 45 to 60 minutes, or until the internal temperature of the fish is between 125 and 130 degrees F. Thirty minutes into the cooking, make the beurre blanc.

To make the beurre blanc, melt 1 tablespoon of the butter in a medium saucepan over medium heat. Add the shallots and stir until soft but not browned (no more than 5 minutes). Reduce the heat slightly if the shallots begin to brown. You don't want them to become crispy or caramelized.

$\longrightarrow$

Add the wine and vinegar and bring to a slight simmer. Let the liquid reduce by half, cooking and stirring for 8 to 10 minutes. The heat will determine how long it will take to reduce; be patient, as you want a somewhat opaque liquid before you add the rest of the butter.

Once the liquid is reduced, turn the burner to the lowest setting. Add the butter 1 tablespoon at a time, whisking to emulsify the butter and the liquid. Don't let it get too hot! Be prepared to move the pan off the heat for a few seconds at a time. You don't want to actually melt the butter, but instead emulsify it into a rich, thick consistency.

When all the butter is added, season with the tarragon and salt. Whisk one more time and then remove from the heat. Serve warm over the salmon. Beurre blanc will stay emulsified for up to 1 hour. If necessary, place the saucepan over the lowest heat while whisking until warm (but not melted or it will separate).

For a family-style meal, pour the sauce over the entire fillet and serve. If serving plated, spoon 1 tablespoon of the sauce over each individual slice of salmon.

WINE PAIRING: The smoked salmon is tender and the rich herbed wine butter sauce creates a full-flavored experience. A full-bodied, oaked chardonnay is fantastic, matching the weight of the dish. But to liven things up and cut through the lush flavors, try a blanc de blancs sparkling wine, a crisp Chablis, or even a sauvignon blanc from the Loire Valley of France. For red, stick to pinot noir.

Beurre Blanc

This classic French sauce is a warm emulsified butter sauce. White wine is reduced with shallots and white wine vinegar, and butter is slowly added to create a creamy and rich sauce to top the salmon. The secret to beurre blanc is not letting the butter fully melt, or separate. The consistency should be similar to a hollandaise sauce.

FROM THE GARDEN:
VEGETARIAN DISHES

The farm-to-table experience in the Pacific Northwest, like coffee, is built into our culture. Access to farmers' markets is all over the region, in cities large and small. Similar to our philosophy on the quality of meat, we seek out the freshest produce. We also know that a large percentage of our customers, readers, and friends are vegetarian, so we have tried to incorporate the same level of flavor and passion into vegetarian dishes to create a culinary experience for everyone.

Many of these recipes are enhanced seasonally when certain vegetables are in their prime (like summer tomatoes), but they can also be cooked year-round. Following is a mix of our favorites that will be a great addition to any menu for yourselves or for your vegetarian friends. The theme for all of our cooking is that if you can cook it inside, you can cook it outside too, with fire. A few of these also make great side dishes, like asparagus and artichokes, and as such won't have a wine pairing because the focus should be on the main items cooked.

GRILLED ARTICHOKES WITH AIOLI

One of Mary's dearest friends, Andrea, introduced us to grilled artichokes. She never disappointed with these artichokes. They may seem intimidating at first, but a simple steam followed by direct grilling creates a tender and flavorful snack. We add a touch of Sweet Rub (page 62) for extra flavor when grilling. And while Andrea used to buy store-bought Dijon aioli to dip the artichokes in, we discovered how easy it can be made on your own.

MAKES 4 ARTICHOKE HALVES (1 HALF PER PERSON)

2 artichokes

Freshly squeezed lemon juice (optional)

2 tablespoons extra-virgin olive oil

1 teaspoon Sweet Rub (page 62)

1 lemon, cut in half down the middle

Basic Aioli, for dipping (page 69)

Dijon mustard (optional)

1 teaspoon Sweet Rub (optional)

Prepare the grill for direct cooking.

To prepare the artichokes, use sharp scissors to cut off the thorny tips of the artichoke leaves. Then cut the artichokes in half lengthwise.

Using a spoon, scoop out and discard the fuzzy portion of the artichoke stem and seed. Scrape out the dark portion so you have just the artichoke flesh. Artichokes will start to turn color when exposed to air, so to prevent this, squeeze lemon juice over the top if desired.

Steam the artichokes for 15 minutes until fork-tender. Remove and set aside.

Coat the artichoke halves with the oil and apply the Sweet Rub to the cut side.

Place the artichokes on the grill leaf side down and cook for 3 minutes. Flip them over to the cut side and grill for 6 to 8 minutes, or until slightly charred.

Place the lemon halves on the grill flesh side down and cook for 6 to 8 minutes, or until the lemon caramelizes. Use the juice of half of that lemon for the Basic Aioli recipe. Reserve the other half for squeezing over the grilled artichokes.

Remove the artichokes from the grill and serve with the Basic Aioli, adding in some extra Dijon mustard and Sweet Rub if desired.

WINE PAIRING: Artichokes are one of those foods that can present a challenge for a wine pairing because of a naturally occurring compound in the artichokes called cynarin, which can make a wine seem sweet. It's best to find a dry wine with high acidity to stand up to the artichokes. Some of our favorites include grüner veltliner, vermintino, and sauvignon blanc.

GRILLED ASPARAGUS WITH SPICY PICKLED PEPPERS

If there's one vegetable we never tire of, it is asparagus, and grilling is the only way to prepare it. The crust that results from grilling brings out a fantastic sweetness. We finish by tossing in some spicy pickled peppers. There's a company out of Portland, Oregon, called Mama Lil's that makes the most addictive and flavorful spicy pickled peppers. Mama Lil's uses Hungarian goathorn peppers. If you can't find them, look for a similar jar of spicy pickled peppers packed in oil. The aromatic oil and spicy peppers complement the crunchy grilled asparagus in the most amazing way. Try to find thick asparagus, as it grills better than thin stalks.

MAKES 4 SERVINGS

1 bunch thick asparagus (⅔ pound)

2 tablespoons extra-virgin olive oil

¼ teaspoon kosher salt

¼ teaspoon freshly ground black pepper

¼ cup chopped spicy pickled peppers

Prepare the grill for direct cooking.

Prepare the asparagus by selecting one and slowly bending it until it snaps. It will break where the woody part ends. Trim the rest of the asparagus to the same length and discard the woody parts. The fresher the asparagus, the less you will have to cut.

Season the asparagus with oil, salt, and pepper, then place on the grill. Grill approximately 5 minutes per side, or until slightly charred, closing the grill cover in between flipping. Flip or rotate at least three times. Keep an eye on the asparagus as this can take less or more time depending on your grill heat and the thickness of the asparagus.

In a large bowl, toss the asparagus, pickled peppers, and some of the pickled pepper oil from the jar. Serve warm.

WINE PAIRING: Similar to artichokes, asparagus can also be a challenge to pair with wine. Add the spicy peppers, and we're doubly challenged. No problem! Grilling asparagus breaks down its strong compounds and makes it more pairing friendly and the peppers give it a kick and acid backbone. Grüner veltliner, semi-dry riesling, and pinot gris/grigio are all favorites with this dish. A fruity Prosecco is pretty dreamy with these asparagus too.

SMOKED TOMATO GAZPACHO

Smoking tomatoes is hands down our favorite way to use up an influx of fresh tomatoes in the summer months. Instead of roasting them in the oven, cook them in the smoker at a very low temperature to soak up that sweet smoke flavor for the most delicious summer gazpacho.

We use smoked tomatoes for everything from a smoked Bloody Mary to smoked marinara sauce to smoked tomato bisque. While gazpacho is traditionally made with fresh raw tomatoes, we're bending the rules a smidge so we can get that lovely smoke infusion. Using a cold smoker will help you avoid cooking the tomatoes, but so does keeping your temperature at 175 to 200 degrees F, allowing the tomatoes to become smoky but not cooked.

MAKES 6 TO 8 SERVINGS

2 pounds tomatoes on the vine (approximately 6 medium tomatoes)

1 medium sweet onion

1 (8-inch) cucumber, peeled, seeded, and roughly chopped

¼ cup good-quality extra-virgin olive oil

2 tablespoons white wine vinegar

½ large jalapeño pepper, roughly chopped

1 large clove garlic, minced

¼ teaspoon kosher salt

Preheat the smoker to 200 degrees F using a fruitwood, like cherry or apple. Avoid mesquite, oak, or hickory; otherwise, the vegetables may pick up too much smoke.

Quarter the tomatoes and onion and place them directly on the grill (or on a baking sheet to pick up any tomato liquid). Cook for 1 hour. Remove and let cool, then peel the skin from the tomatoes.

In a food processor, pulse the tomatoes, onion, cucumber, oil, vinegar, jalapeño, garlic, and salt to the desired consistency.

Serve cold with a drizzle of good-quality extra-virgin olive oil and garnish with chopped cucumber and red bell pepper.

WINE PAIRING: Maybe because this is a fantastic summertime meal or maybe because of our affinity for rosé, but this meal is just *made* for a fruity and full-flavored rosé.

GRILLED BEET CITRUS SALAD

Sean loves beets. He's not much into green salads, so this one is meant to be heavy on the beets, with just enough greens for balance and crunch. Beets are very firm when raw, so we take the liberty of roasting them in the oven to soften, then finish them on the hot grill for flavor and char. The beets can be roasted the day before and kept in the refrigerator until time to grill, making this an easy party dish. While beets can be an earthy flavor on their own, adding citrus really brightens up the vegetable quite well. This works great with both red and golden beets.

MAKES 4 TO 6 SERVINGS

For the beet salad
- 1 pound red beets
- ¼ cup chevre cheese
- 2 cups mixed salad greens
- ¼ cup Smoked Pickled Onions (page 122)
- Parmesan cheese, for garnish
- Pinch of finishing salt
- Shaved smoked almonds (optional)

For the orange vinaigrette
- 2 tablespoons freshly squeezed orange juice
- 2 tablespoons red wine vinegar
- 2 teaspoons Dijon mustard
- 1 teaspoon honey
- ⅛ teaspoon kosher salt
- ¼ cup extra-virgin olive oil

Preheat the oven to 400 degrees F.

To prepare the beets, trim off the stems and roots. Clean the beets, then wrap in aluminum foil and place on a baking sheet. Add a small amount of water to the pan and place in the oven.

Roast the beets for up to 60 minutes. Smaller beets will likely be done earlier; they're done when you can insert a fork easily. If necessary, continue cooking until fork-tender and add more water to the pan if needed.

Let the beets cool, then remove the skins. Use gloves when removing the skin; otherwise, expect your fingers to turn red. If making a day ahead, refrigerate the beets.

To make the vinaigrette, in a large bowl, combine the orange juice, vinegar, Dijon, honey, and salt. Slowly whisk in the oil to emulsify. Set aside.

Prepare the grill for direct cooking.

$\longrightarrow$

Cut the beets in half, then place them on the grill for 8 minutes per side, or until slightly charred. Remove the beets, then cut them in half again, quartering the beets for final presentation. (If you quarter them before grilling, some beets may fall through the grates.)

To the bowl with the vinaigrette, add the beets and toss. Add the chevre. Stir again, gently, and add the greens and pickled onions. Toss one more time, then plate.

Add Parmesan shavings to each serving, sprinkle a pinch of finishing salt over the top, and add the almonds for crunch.

WINE PAIRING: Medium-bodied rosés, such as those from southern France, Italy, and Oregon, work very well with grilled beets. Similarly, sparkling rosé is super refreshing with this salad. If you're craving red, cabernet franc from the Loire Valley of France pairs surprisingly well with the earthy beets.

SMOKED BABA GHANOUSH

The first wine business trip Mary was invited to go on was to Santorini. This Greek island had been on her bucket list since she was a little girl, so she felt like she hit the jackpot on the first try. To this day, it remains one of the most memorable experiences of her life. The food, the scenery, the wine! There was even one restaurant that had the most memorable smoked ice cream. She was in heaven! Plus, baba ghanoush and the freshest tomatoes were served daily, and she recalls them being so simple yet so delicious. There had to be a way to keep the memory of this trip alive. Thus . . .

MAKES 1½ CUPS

2 medium eggplants, halved lengthwise and tops removed (see note)

1 teaspoon kosher salt, divided

⅓ cup roughly chopped fresh Italian parsley, plus more for garnish (optional)

⅓ cup good-quality extra-virgin olive oil, plus more for garnish (optional)

¼ cup tahini

3 tablespoons freshly squeezed lemon juice

2 cloves garlic, roughly chopped

Cracked black pepper, to taste

Smoked salt, for garnish (optional)

Smoked paprika, for garnish (optional)

Season the flesh side of the eggplant halves with ½ teaspoon of the salt.

Place the eggplants on a rimmed baking sheet, skin side up to allow the water that will be drawn out of the eggplants to drip onto the sheet. Refrigerate for up to 2 hours.

Preheat the smoker to 250 degrees F using applewood.

Place the eggplants on the smoker, skin side down, for 1 hour to 90 minutes, or until the outer skin begins to brown and the texture is soft when inserting a toothpick or sharp knife (the outer skin will still be a bit tough). If the texture isn't soft after 1 hour, feel free to increase the temperature to 275 to 300 degrees F until it softens enough to process (no more than 2 hours of total cooking time). Remove from the smoker.

When the eggplants are cool enough to work with, spoon out the flesh and put it in a food processor. (You could also use a sharp knife to remove the outer skin.)

Add the remaining ½ teaspoon of salt, parsley, oil, tahini, lemon juice, garlic, and pepper to the food processor. Pulse until you reach a texture you like. Some like it a bit chunky, but we prefer it silky smooth. Add more oil if it appears too dry or is too thick. Adjust the ingredients to taste.

$\longrightarrow$

Pour dip into a serving dish or bowl. Top with your preferred garnishes. Serve with pita bread, baguette slices, or crackers.

NOTE: Eggplant: size matters. The really large ones can be bitter and full of big, dark seeds. Avoid these, or be prepared to remove some of the seeds after smoking.

If you still see lots of large, dark seeds after cooking the eggplant, remove them before making the dip. They will contribute a bitter, unpleasant taste.

Avoid wrinkled, bruised, or damaged eggplant. It should feel firm, smooth, and spring back slightly upon touch.

Use it fresh. Eggplant will keep for a couple days in a dry location (avoid the fridge because it's too cold), but ideally it should be used immediately.

Cook eggplant until it's soft. If it doesn't get soft after 1 hour on your smoker, increase the temperature and continue cooking until it does.

WINE PAIRING: The island of Santorini, which inspired this recipe, is all about assyrtiko, a highly acidic dry white wine that is fantastic with baba ghanoush. But assyrtiko can be challenging to find. Easier to find but equally great with this dish is Chablis, which balances the fresh lemon flavors. For red, choose something light, like a pinot noir.

PULLED MUSHROOM SLIDERS

We should all eat more veggies. That's easier to accomplish when you can substitute vegetables in meals that meat eaters enjoy, like pulled mushroom sliders instead of pulled pork. And the bonus we have is that Oregon is mushroom heaven.

When looking for the perfect mushrooms to mimic pulled pork, ideally you want ones with the thickest stems you can find. The best are giant king oysters, but they are hard to locate and they're expensive. The best substitute is to use the largest white button mushrooms available. We're going to repeat: look for the biggest white mushrooms you can find with thick stems. The stems pull just like shredded meat, but the caps do pretty well too.

While there's no true substitute for the flavor of pulled pork, these sliders are meaty, smoky, and full of incredible flavors. Even hardcore carnivores devour these!

MAKES 8 TO 10 SLIDERS

2 pounds large white button or king oyster mushrooms with thick, large stems

¼ cup plus 1 tablespoon extra-virgin olive oil

¼ cup Sweet Rub (page 62)

½ cup Pinot Noir BBQ Sauce (page 66) or your favorite Kansas City–style sauce

1 package soft slider buns (such as King's Hawaiian)

½ cup Smoked Pickled Onions (page 122)

1 cup prepared coleslaw

Preheat the smoker to 225 degrees F using applewood or oakwood.

Clean any dirt off the mushrooms with a moist paper towel (leave the stems on).

On a large baking sheet, season the mushrooms with ¼ cup of the oil and the Sweet Rub. Place the baking sheet on the smoker for 1 hour, or until the mushrooms are soft and slightly browned.

Remove the mushrooms from the smoker and let cool enough to handle.

Using your hands, remove the stems from the caps and squeeze out and discard any liquid that has pooled up inside the caps. (If you don't squeeze out the liquid, the texture of the mushrooms may be slimy.) Using two forks, shred the caps and stems, as you would shred chicken.

$\longrightarrow$

In a large cast-iron skillet over medium-high heat, add the remaining 1 tablespoon oil and the mushrooms. Cook for 5 minutes, moving them minimally in order to crisp the mushrooms. If they haven't crisped after 5 minutes, cook another 3 to 4 minutes, tossing only once or twice, until you see a little crispiness develop. Add the Pinot Noir BBQ Sauce, mix, and cook 1 to 2 minutes to caramelize.

Remove from the heat. Serve on a soft slider bun with the Smoked Pickled Onions and the coleslaw. Top with any remaining sauce and enjoy warm.

WINE PAIRING: Mushrooms have rich and meaty flavors and textures, and they take the smoke flavor quite well. With the caramelized BBQ sauce, these sliders are fantastic candidates to pair with a cabernet franc, syrah, and even zinfandel. Or if you're looking for something refreshing to offset the richness of the dish, a bold rosé will never let you down.

SWISS CHARD AND HAZELNUT GRILLED VEGGIE PATTIES

Cooking at events always challenges us to come up with unique items for our vegetarian friends and customers, and people get tired of generic black bean burgers fast! Living on a hazelnut farm, we came up with the idea to create a patty incorporating hazelnuts, one that has the texture and flavor needed to stand up to the grill yet remains a tasty option that people would not only eat but crave. The good news is you don't have to have a hazelnut farm to enjoy these meat-free burgers, as hazelnut flour is easy to find. This recipe was inspired by chef, friend, and sausage maker extraordinaire Adam Ruplinger. The veggie patty has a unusual combination of flavors and textures, giving it the ability to stay firm while grilling.

MAKES 4 (5-OUNCE) PATTIES

2 tablespoons extra-virgin olive oil

1½ cups finely diced yellow onion

2 cloves garlic, minced

1 bunch Swiss chard, destemmed and finely chopped

2 cups hazelnut flour

¾ cup panko bread crumbs

5 ounces shredded pepper jack cheese

¼ cup tahini

2 eggs

3 tablespoons nutritional yeast

½ teaspoon dried oregano

½ teaspoon kosher salt

½ teaspoon coarse ground black pepper

4 slices pepper jack cheese (optional)

In a large skillet over medium heat, add the oil and then the onions and cook for 5 to 7 minutes, or until the onions are tender and translucent but not caramelized. Add the garlic and cook for 2 minutes. Add the Swiss chard, then turn the heat to low. Sauté until the chard is wilted but not overcooked, 6 to 8 minutes. Allow to cool.

In a large bowl, combine the flour, bread crumbs, cheese, tahini, eggs, yeast, oregano, salt, and pepper. Add the Swiss chard mix and combine by hand. It will come together in a firm doughlike texture.

Using your hands, form the mixture into 4 patties. If you want uniform patties, oil a 3½-inch-wide ramekin (or 3½-inch top of an airtight jar), fill with the mixture halfway, and press firmly. Tap several times on a cutting board to release the patty.

Prepare the grill for direct cooking.

Place the patties over direct heat and grill for 4 to 6 minutes, or until a nice sear develops. Flip and add cheese, if desired. Cook for another 4 to 6 minutes, until a sear develops, and remove from the grill.

To assemble the patties into a burger, follow the assembly instructions for Smokehouse Burgers on page 134.

WINE PAIRING: The flavor of the patties is quite mild, so the pairing is going to be determined by your toppings. Do you go ketchup or stick with a creamy mayo? Cheese or no cheese? A safe go-to wine for either would be rosé, but if you're craving red, a fruity Beaujolais (made from gamay) works great. For white, opt for torrontés, viognier, or Rhône-style white blends.

SMOKED TOFU BURNT ENDS

Mary loves thinking outside the box with BBQ, and likes to recreate classics with nontraditional ingredients, like swapping tofu for beef in the classic "burnt ends". The tofu firms up nicely in the smoker, infuses with sweet smoke, and has great savory flavors from the miso marinade. This is a fantastic weeknight meal served with rice and vegetables or as a side dish. This is a good one to have in your arsenal for your vegetarian friends come summer cookout season.

MAKES 4 SERVINGS AS AN APPETIZER OR SNACK

For the tofu
- 1 (14-ounce) package extra-firm tofu, drained
- 2 tablespoons Sweet Rub (page 62)
- ½ cup Pinot Noir BBQ Sauce (page 66)

For the marinade
- ¼ cup brown miso paste
- ¼ cup apple cider vinegar
- ¼ cup extra-virgin olive oil

To prepare the tofu, cut the tofu in half vertically, place on a wire cooling rack, cover with a clean kitchen towel, and place a cutting board over the top. On top of the cutting board, put a heavy pan (cast iron works well) or 28-ounce cans of anything. Place in the fridge and let the liquid press out for a minimum of 1 hour (or up to 3 hours). Squeezing out the liquid will allow the tofu to absorb the marinade.

Remove the tofu from the refrigerator, then cut into 1-inch cubes.

To make the marinade, in a small bowl, whisk together the miso, vinegar, and oil. Put the marinade into a 1-gallon ziplock bag. Add the tofu. Seal the bag, removing as much air as possible. Marinate in the refrigerator for 1 hour.

Preheat the smoker to 225 degrees F using applewood or cherrywood.

Place the tofu on a wire cooling rack and sprinkle with the dry rub, then put it into the smoker for 2 hours and 30 minutes to 3 hours.

The tofu is done when it starts to turn a darker color and has a slightly firm texture. Remove the tofu from the smoker and toss with the Pinot Noir BBQ Sauce in medium bowl. Place the bowl onto the wire rack and into the smoker for 30 minutes to let the sauce set. Remove from the smoker and enjoy.

WINE PAIRING: Tofu is a blank canvas. The flavor here is all sweet smoke and the BBQ sauce. Go with those sauce flavors and opt for a barbera, zinfandel, or even a syrah or cabernet franc.

PORTOBELLO MUSHROOM BURGERS

Portobello mushrooms are hearty and satisfying (even for a hardcore meat lover). These burgers are jam-packed with flavor from a savory marinade, a slow smoke, and a spicy chipotle aioli sauce. Make sure to stack your burgers two high per serving to give them more balance. The mushrooms shrink while cooking, so a single one could get lost between a bun and the great mayo.

MAKES 2 BURGERS

For the marinade
⅓ cup extra-virgin olive oil
¼ cup Worcestershire sauce
2 tablespoons minced shallots
2 cloves garlic, minced

For the mushrooms
4 portobello mushrooms
2 teaspoons Sweet Rub (page 62)

For the aioli
½ cup good-quality mayonnaise
1 tablespoon chipotle adobo sauce (if you don't like heat, use 1 teaspoon)
1 chipotle pepper, finely diced
2 teaspoons freshly squeezed lemon juice

For the burgers
2 soft pretzel buns
¼ cup Smoked Pickled Onions (page 122)
1 bunch red leaf lettuce
1 large heirloom or beefsteak tomato, sliced

To make the marinade, combine the oil, Worcestershire, shallots, and garlic in a 1-gallon ziplock bag. Remove the gills from the mushrooms using a spoon. Add the mushrooms to the bag and seal, tossing to coat the mushrooms thoroughly. Place in the refrigerator to marinate for 30 minutes.

Preheat the smoker to 225 degrees F using applewood.

To cook the mushrooms, remove the mushrooms from the marinade and discard the marinade. Apply ½ teaspoon of the Sweet Rub per mushroom cap on both sides. Depending on the size of your mushrooms, you may need a smidge more or less.

Place the mushrooms directly on the smoker and cook for 1 hour, or until the mushrooms are soft. They will turn a dark color and shrink. Remove from grill.

Make the chipotle aioli prior to assembling the burgers. In a small bowl, combine the mayonnaise, adobo sauce, chipotle pepper, and lemon juice and mix.

To assemble the burgers, place 2 mushrooms on the bottom bun, then top with the sauce, Smoked Pickled Onions, lettuce, tomato, and top bun.

WINE PAIRING: This is a good one for a classic Bordeaux blend. Or for a hit of something fruity, reach for a Washington State merlot.

A SIDE PROJECT

Sides should complement the main course. When considering sides, you don't need to overdo it by making too many. Instead, pick and choose side dishes based upon the season (hot summer equals cold sides; cool weather equals warm, comforting sides), as well as the ability to use a side in multiple dishes, like our Smoked Pickled Onions (page 122; they're great on everything from burgers to tacos).

Some of the side dishes in this chapter don't have a wine pairing, as they are meant to be complements to the star, the main entree. But the wine pairings do follow the same rules of contrast and complement. Make sure the wine you choose for the main dish also works for the side dish, or adjust the side accordingly.

GRILLED CORN WITH SMOKED HONEY BUTTER

Grilled corn is something our family could eat every day of the week. And serving the ears with smoked honey butter is the icing on the cake. This is such a delightful and delicious way to cook corn.

MAKES 6 EARS OF CORN

6 ears sweet corn, shucked

6 tablespoons Smoked Honey Butter (page 177)

Finishing salt

Prepare the grill for direct/indirect cooking.

Place the corn on the grill over direct heat. Cover and cook, turning the corn every 4 minutes to prevent charring. Close the lid in between turns to keep the flame from getting too large. If the flame gets high, turn the corn more often, then move it to the indirect heat, cover, and finish.

Remove the corn from the grill when lightly charred and soft, 16 to 20 minutes total. Immediately place 1 tablespoon of the Smoked Honey Butter on each ear and spread evenly.

Sprinkle finishing salt to taste over the corn and enjoy.

TRUFFLE POTATO GRATIN

In Portland, it seems we truffle everything. But seriously, adding truffle to a gratin is legit. We add a little cream and cook it on our grill. The result is a very indulgent side. Don't be alarmed by all the dairy—just enjoy it.

MAKES 4 TO 6 SERVINGS

2 pounds Yukon gold potatoes (about 4 medium potatoes)

1½ cups heavy cream

1 cup whole milk

¼ cup shredded white onion

1 large clove garlic, minced

1 tablespoon truffle oil (plus more for drizzling)

1 teaspoon kosher salt

1 teaspoon chopped fresh thyme

Unsalted butter, for the pan

1 cup grated Parmesan cheese

1 cup grated Gruyère or Asiago cheese

Prepare the grill for direct/indirect cooking with a target temperature of 375 degrees F.

Using a mandolin, cut the potatoes into ⅛-inch-thick slices. Set aside.

In a large bowl, whisk the cream, milk, onion, garlic, oil, salt, and thyme. Add the potatoes. Using your hands, incorporate the liquid mixture and the potatoes.

Butter the bottom and sides of a large cast-iron pan. Fan out the potatoes in the pan in layers, like shingles on a roof. After the first layer of potatoes, add ¼ cup of the Parmesan. Continue in this manner for three more layers, then top with the remaining ¼ cup Parmesan and the Gruyère.

Carefully pour the liquid mixture into the pan and cover.

Place the pan on the indirect side of the grill (to prevent the bottom layer from scorching), cover the grill, and cook for 60 minutes.

Remove the cover of the gratin and cook for another 10 minutes, or until the cheese is browning and the potatoes are soft.

Remove from the grill and let rest for 10 minutes to allow the pan to cool. Drizzle with more truffle oil and serve.

SMOKED POBLANO MAC AND CHEESE

This is a rich and creamy mac and cheese with a mix of cheeses plus a bit of heat. The smoked cheese and poblano peppers give the dish sweet and earthy flavors. You can cook the dish directly on the grill, giving it even more incredible flavor. This is rich, ooey, gooey, comfort food at its finest!

MAKES 6 SERVINGS

For the smoked poblano peppers
- 4 poblano peppers, cut in half and seeds removed

For the mac and cheese
- 2 cups uncooked pasta (macaroni, elbow, or other small pasta with a hollow shape works well)
- 4 tablespoons unsalted butter
- 4 tablespoons all-purpose flour
- 3 cups whole milk
- 1 cup shredded sharp cheddar
- 1 cup shredded smoked cheddar
- ½ cup crème fraîche
- 1 tablespoon Dijon mustard
- 1 teaspoon kosher salt, divided
- ½ teaspoon ground nutmeg
- ¼ cup panko bread crumbs
- ½ teaspoon smoked paprika

To make the smoked peppers, preheat the smoker to 250 degrees F using cherrywood.

Place the peppers on the smoker for 1 hour, or until soft and tender. Remove them from the smoker, and dice them. (This can be done in advance.)

To make the mac and cheese, prepare the grill for direct/indirect cooking.

In a large stockpot, cook the pasta for a few minutes less than the package instructions recommend (you want the pasta to be a little undercooked). Drain, and set aside.

In a large saucepan over medium heat, melt the butter. Add the flour, and stir until smooth. Continue cooking and stirring for 2 to 3 minutes, or until the mixture starts to turn a golden color. Slowly add the milk, 1 cup at a time, and whisk to combine. Continue whisking until the sauce starts to thicken, approximately 4 to 5 minutes.

Remove the saucepan from heat and add the cheeses, crème fraîche, Dijon, ½ teaspoon of the salt, nutmeg, and the smoked poblano peppers. Mix until creamy.

Mix in the pasta, then transfer to a 9-inch round cast-iron skillet. Top with the bread crumbs, the remaining ½ teaspoon of salt, and smoked paprika.

Place the skillet on the grill over indirect heat, and cook for 20 minutes, or until the cheeses are melted and starting to brown. (Alternatively, you can cook this in the oven set to 350 degrees F). Remove and serve.

NOTE: When grilling with high heat, even if indirect, avoid using glass dishes. They tend to break due to the heat. Cast iron is preferred because stainless steel will discolor from the heat and smoke.

SMOKED PUMPKIN RISOTTO

On a trip to northeast Italy's Veneto region a few years ago, Mary noticed that many of the restaurants offered not just risotto on the menu but pumpkin risotto. It was late fall and they were all taking advantage of this late-harvest squash in the greatest way possible. The pumpkin added such creaminess and flavor to this traditional arborio rice dish that we had to try it with smoked pumpkin back at home. Our version adds a lovely sweetness and just a kiss of smoke flavor. Feel free to use Smoked Chicken Stock (page 94) for even more smoky goodness.

MAKES 4 TO 6 SERVINGS

For the smoked pumpkin and bacon
1 small yellow or sugar pumpkin (3 to 4 pounds), quartered and seeds removed
6 slices thick-cut bacon

For the fried sage
1 tablespoon unsalted butter
6 to 8 leaves fresh sage
Kosher salt

For the risotto
5 to 6 cups chicken stock (Smoked Chicken Stock on page 94, or store-bought)

2 tablespoons unsalted butter
1 small onion, chopped
1 large clove garlic, minced
6 sprigs fresh thyme
1½ cups uncooked arborio rice
¾ cup dry white wine
½ teaspoon kosher salt
¼ teaspoon coarse ground black pepper
Pinch of ground nutmeg
¾ cup shredded Parmesan cheese

To make the smoked pumpkin and bacon, preheat the smoker to 225 degrees F.

Place the pumpkin quarters on the smoker, skin side down. Place the bacon on the smoker, and smoke both for 1 hour. Remove the bacon if it has fully cooked and looks crispy. Crumble the bacon and set it aside.

Increase the temperature to 300 degrees F, and continue cooking the pumpkin for 30 to 60 minutes, or until it is fork-tender. Remove from the smoker. When the pumpkin is cool enough to handle, spoon out the flesh and puree it in a food processor. (Depending on the size of the pumpkin, this should yield 3 to 4 cups of puree. Reserve 1½ cups for the risotto.)

To make the fried sage, in a small saucepan over medium heat, melt the butter. Add the sage leaves and fry for 2 to 3 minutes, or until crispy. Place the leaves on a paper towel to remove excess butter. Sprinkle with a touch of salt, or to taste.

To make the risotto, in a medium saucepan over medium heat, heat the chicken stock and then bring down to a light simmer.

→

In a large, heavy saucepan, melt the butter and then add the onion. Cook for 5 minutes, or until tender. Add the garlic and thyme and cook for 1 minute. Add the rice and stir just to coat with the onion mixture and slightly toast the rice. Add the wine and simmer for 1 to 2 minutes, or until the rice has absorbed the liquid.

Next, add 1 ladle of the simmering broth and ¼ cup of the pumpkin puree. Slowly stir until it has been absorbed, about 3 minutes. Continue adding 1 ladle of the broth and ¼ cup of the puree at a time, stirring constantly, until all the rice has been cooked and is tender. This should take 25 to 30 minutes total. The risotto should be creamy and the rice a bit al dente. Add the salt and pepper (or more to taste) and the nutmeg (more or less depending on how you like the flavor). Turn off the heat. Stir in the Parmesan. Top with the fried sage and bacon crumbles and serve immediately.

Variation

Alternatively, you can peel and cube the pumpkin, toss on a baking sheet, and place in the smoker. This will speed up the roasting process and allow more smoke infusion into the pumpkin.

To make a vegetarian-friendly version, substitute vegetable stock for the chicken stock and eliminate the bacon.

DIJON POTATO SALAD

We've never been fans of rich, mayo-based potato salads. In this salad, we love the combination of Dijon and the zing of apple cider vinegar. That said, this simple side is still meant to have focused flavors: the light zing and texture of the whole grain mustard, the crunch from the green onions, and the sour-sweet bite of the apple cider vinegar. This is a great salad to make the day before a big cook so you can just pull it from the refrigerator and serve. It also works better for potlucks, where the food sits out on a blazing-hot day.

MAKES 4 TO 6 SERVINGS

1½ pounds Yukon gold potatoes, cleaned and dried

2 tablespoons plus ¼ teaspoon kosher salt

¼ cup apple cider vinegar

¼ cup extra-virgin olive oil

1 tablespoon whole grain Dijon mustard

¼ teaspoon coarse ground black pepper

½ cup chopped green onions

Slice the potatoes into 1-inch bite-size portions. In a large pot, add the potatoes, enough water to cover, and 2 tablespoons of the salt and bring to a boil. Reduce to a simmer and cook for 12 minutes, or until the potatoes are fork-tender but not mushy. Pour them into a colander and set aside.

In a large bowl, add the vinegar, oil, mustard, the remaining ¼ teaspoon of salt, and pepper. Whisk to combine. Add the potatoes and green onions. Stir the potatoes a few times to coat with the dressing.

As the potatoes cool, they will draw in the extra liquid. Serve the salad warm or cold. It will keep in the refrigerator for up to 3 days.

ACKNOWLEDGMENTS

What an amazing journey! We are eternally grateful to all who helped make our first cookbook happen, including:

To Yolanda Cressler and Pat Martin. This book couldn't have been completed with two 8-year-olds running amuck. Your superstar talents as grandmothers allowed us to do our thing. Thank you for always being here for us!

To Mary's sister, Serenity, as the better writer in the family, for proofing our work and teaching us your grammatical ways.

To all of our amazing friends and neighbors (you know who you are!) who have been our taste testers over the years. To Adam Ruplinger, for your mentorship, friendship, and culinary talent.

To Snake River Farms and Carlton Farms for providing all the gorgeous meat for the photos in this book. To Dina Avila and Anne Parker for bringing our recipes to life through your photography and styling.

To Dianne Jacob, for helping us bring this story to life through your coaching, and Martha Hopkins for helping us find the right partner to publish it!

To our incredible team at Sasquatch: Gary Luke, Tony Ong, Jill Saginario, Nikki Sprinkle, Molly Woolbright, Diane Sinitsky, and Steven Blaski. You've been a true pleasure to work with. It's been the coolest experience watching these words turn into a gorgeous book.

To the customers who have supported our catering work with Ember and Vine over the years.

And, finally, to our Vindulge readers! None of this could have happened without your readership and support! This book is for you.

INDEX

Note: Page numbers in *italic* refer to photographs.

To Dad: you would have loved this! —MC

To Cole and Sawyer, our pitmasters in training. —SM

Printed in China

SASQUATCH BOOKS with colophon is a registered trademark of Penguin Random House LLC

24 23 22 21 20   9 8 7 6 5 4 3 2 1

Editor: Gary Luke | Production editor: Jill Saginario | Designer: Tony Ong
Cover and interior photography: Dina Avila | Food styling: Anne Parker
Supplemental photography: Mary Cressler, with the exception of pages 60, 110, and 160: © iStock.com/Nastco; pages 70 and 194: © Annie Spratt; pages 90 and 174: © Michael Mroczek; pages 138, 212 (and wood effect end papers): © iStock.com/Nevodka
Author photograph: Del Munroe

Library of Congress Cataloging-in-Publication Data
Names: Cressler, Mary, author. | Martin, Sean, 1975- author.
Title: Fire & wine : 75 smoke-infused recipes from the grill with perfect
  wine pairings / Mary Cressler and Sean Martin.
Other titles: Fire and wine
Description: Seattle, WA : Sasquatch Books, [2020] | Includes index.
  Identifiers: LCCN 2019022799 (print) | LCCN 2019022800 (ebook) | ISBN
  9781632172778 (hardcover) | ISBN 9781632172785 (ebook)
Subjects: LCSH: Barbecuing. | Wine selection. | LCGFT: Cookbooks.
Classification: LCC TX840.B3 C74 2020 (print) | LCC TX840.B3 (ebook) |
  DDC 641.7/6--dc23
LC record available at https://lccn.loc.gov/2019022799
LC ebook record available at https://lccn.loc.gov/2019022800

ISBN: 978-1-63217-277-8

Sasquatch Books
1904 Third Avenue, Suite 710
Seattle, WA 98101

SasquatchBooks.com

MARY CRESSLER and **SEAN MARTIN** blog about
BBQ and wine on their website, Vindulge, which received
an IACP nomination for Best Recipe-Based Blog in 2017.
In 2016 their website won Best Original Photography
from the Wine Blog Awards, as well as a nomination for
Best Overall Wine Blog. Mary is a certified sommelier,
recipe developer, and food writer with credits in *Wine
Enthusiast, Serious Eats,* Weber.com, and more, and she
is also a frequent judge for wine competitions. Mary and
Sean founded Ember and Vine, an award-winning catering
and events firm specializing in wood-fired cooking, and
are also frequent guests on Portland's morning television
show, *AM Northwest*. Mary and Sean teach classes on wine
and cooking. They live on a hazelnut farm in Oregon wine
country with their sweet and energetic twin boys.